HOW 2 Be
AWSUM

AWSUM

A LOLcat Guide 2 Life

GOTHAM BOOKS

GOTHAM BOOKS
Published by Penguin Group (USA) Inc.
375 Hudson Street, New York, New York 10014, U.S.A.

Penguin Group (Canada), 90 Eglinton Avenue East, Suite 700, Toronto, Ontario M4P 2Y3, Canada (a division of Pearson Penguin Canada Inc.); Penguin Books Ltd, 80 Strand, London WC2R ORL, England; Penguin Ireland, 25 St Stephen's Green, Dublin 2, Ireland (a division of Penguin Books Ltd); Penguin Group (Australia), 250 Camberwell Road, Camberwell, Victoria 3124, Australia (a division of Pearson Australia Group Pty Ltd); Penguin Books India Pvt Ltd, 11 Community Centre, Panchsheel Park, New Delhi - 110 017, India; Penguin Group (NZ), 67 Apollo Drive, Rosedale, North Shore 0632, New Zealand (a division of Pearson New Zealand Ltd); Penguin Books (South Africa) (Pty) Ltd, 24 Sturdee Avenue, Rosebank, Johannesburg 2196, South Africa

Penguin Books Ltd, Registered Offices: 80 Strand, London WC2R ORL, England

Published by Gotham Books, a member of Penguin Group (USA) Inc.

First printing, November 2011

3   5   7   9   10   8   6   4

Gotham Books and the skyscraper logo are trademarks of Penguin Group (USA) Inc.

Library of Congress Cataloging-in-Publication Data

How 2 be awsum : a LOLcat guide 2 life / Professor Happycat and icanhascheezburger.com.
p. cm.
Includes bibliographical references and index.
ISBN 978-1-592-40702-6 (pbk. : alk. paper)
1. Cats--Humor. I. Professor Happycat. II. icanhascheezburger.com.
PN6231.C23H686 2011
818'.602--dc23
2011032727

Printed in teh United States of America
Set in IMPACT!!1!
Designed bai Kelsie Kaufman
Illustrations bai Joe Rufa

No kittehs were harmd in teh making of dis book.

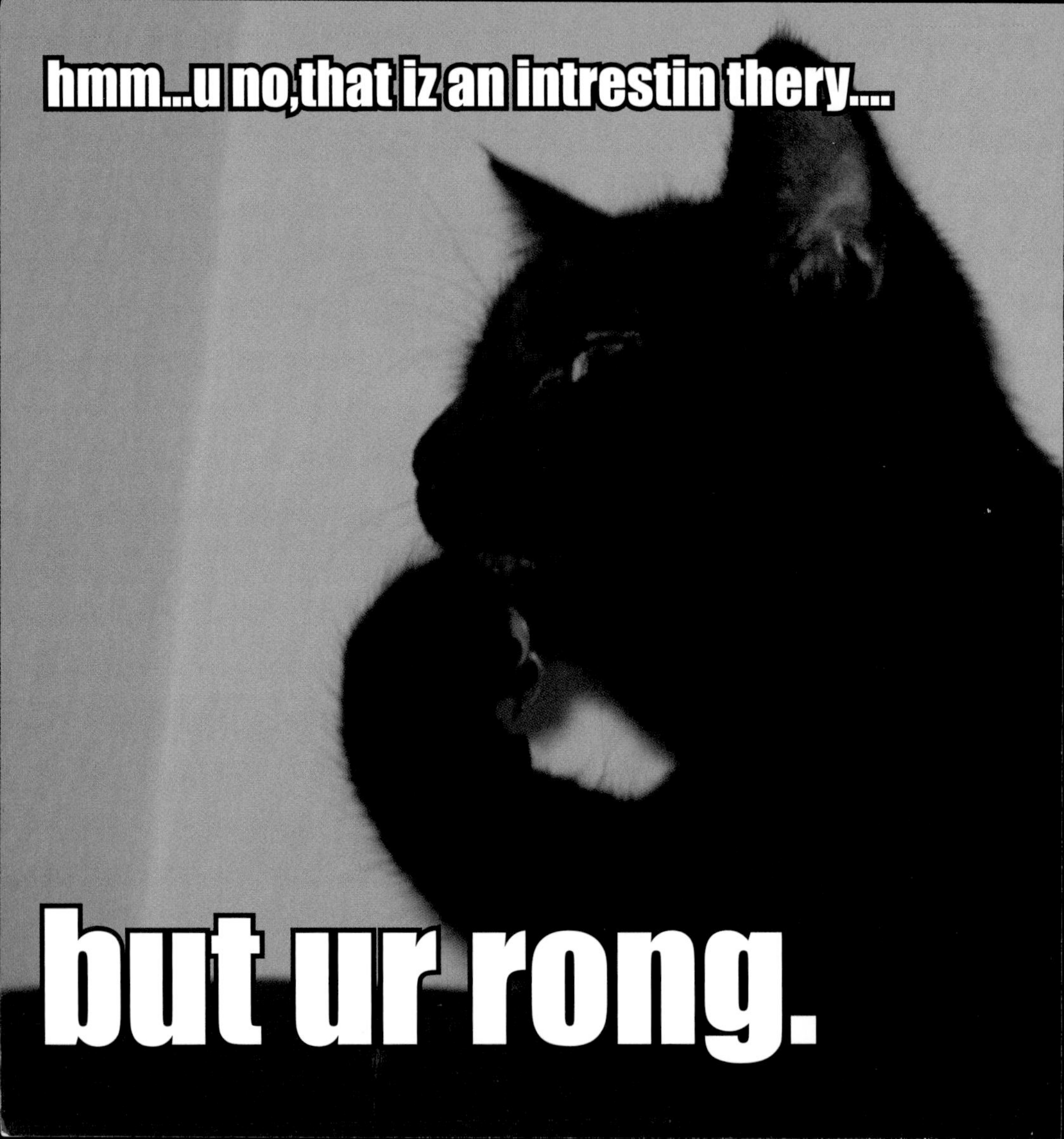
hmm...u no,that iz an intrestin thery....
but ur rong.

Shakespeare Kitteh

Dost not approve of thou foul grammar

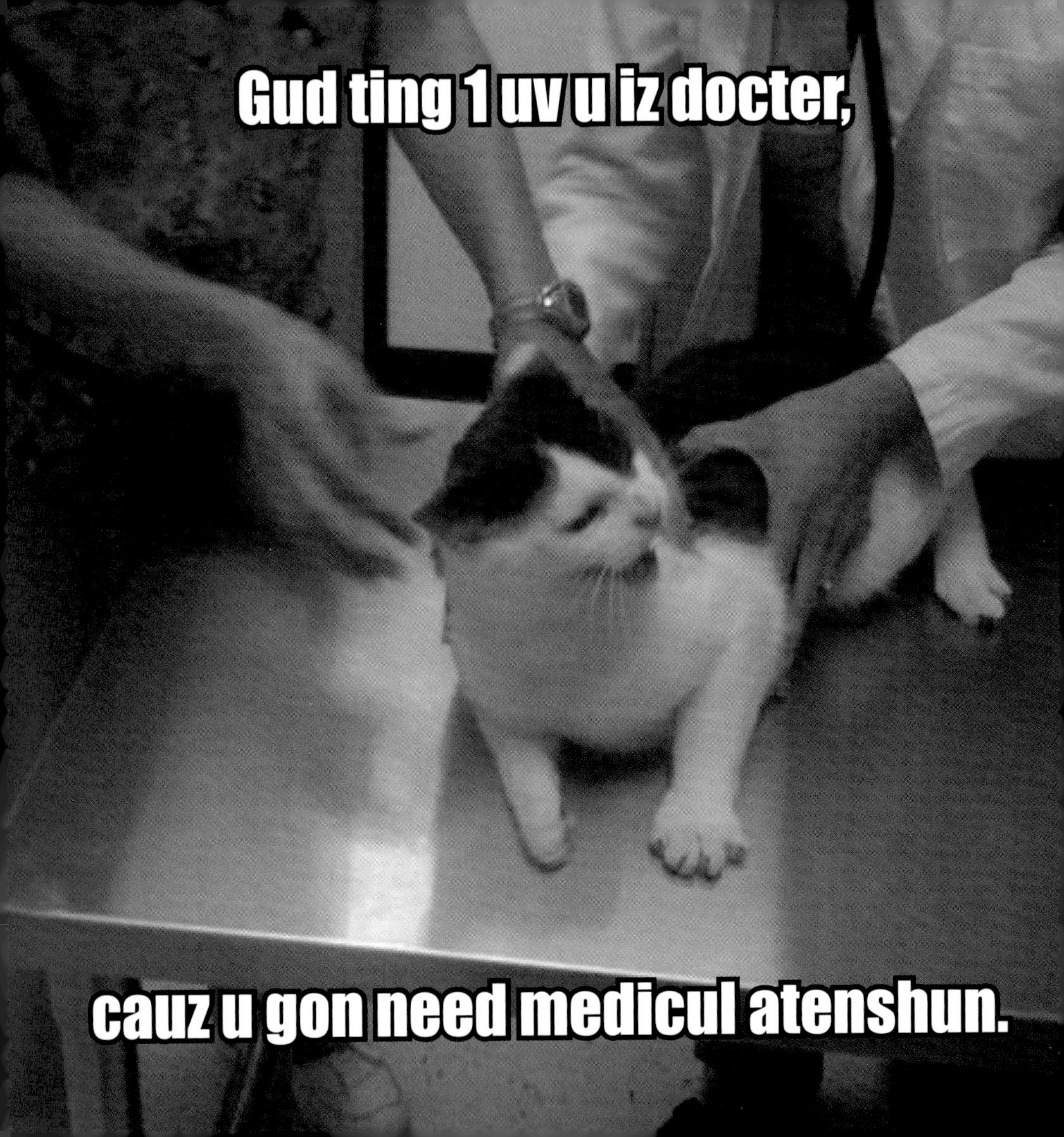
Gud ting 1 uv u iz docter,
cauz u gon need medicul atenshun.

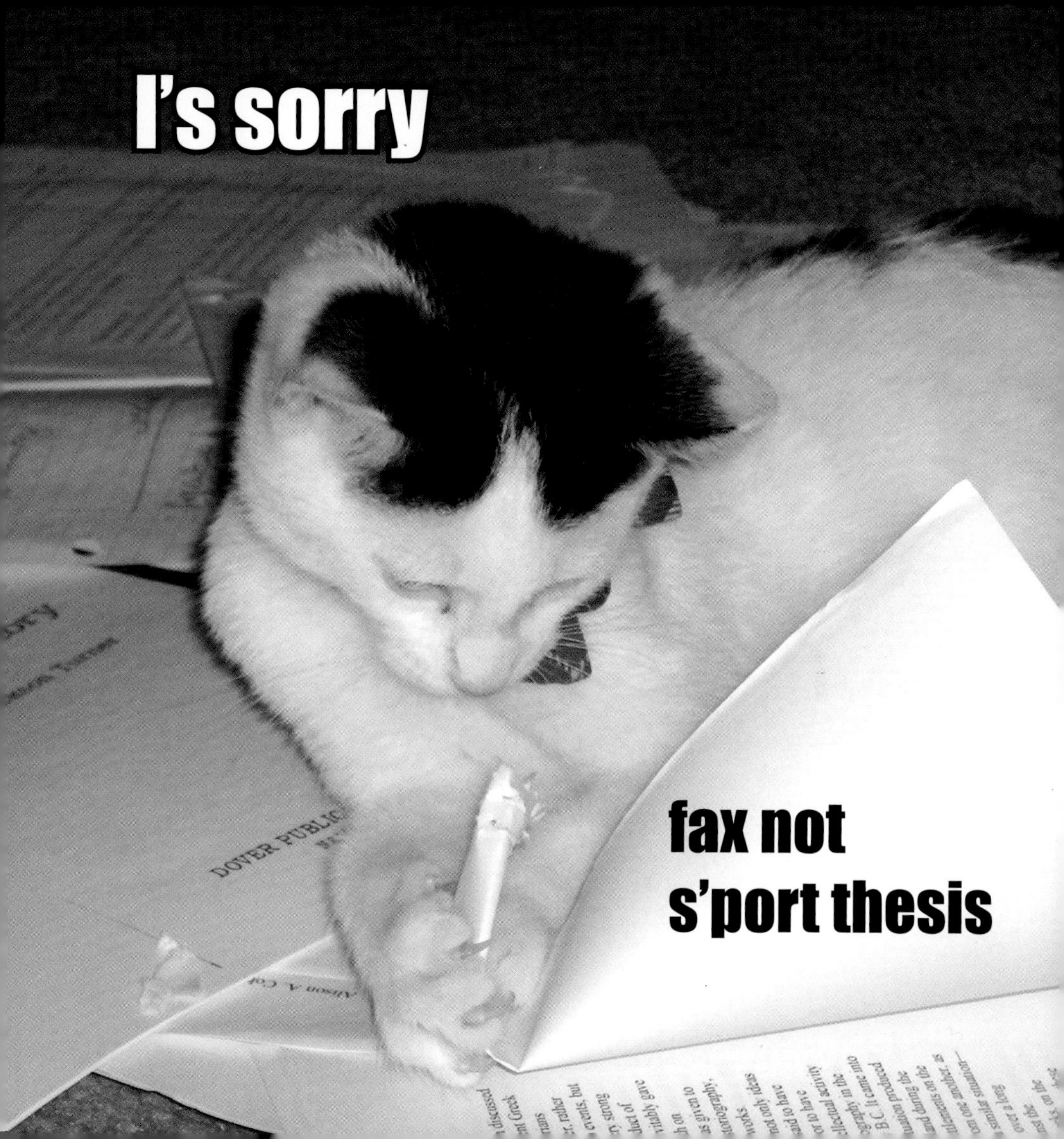
I's sorry
fax not
s'port thesis

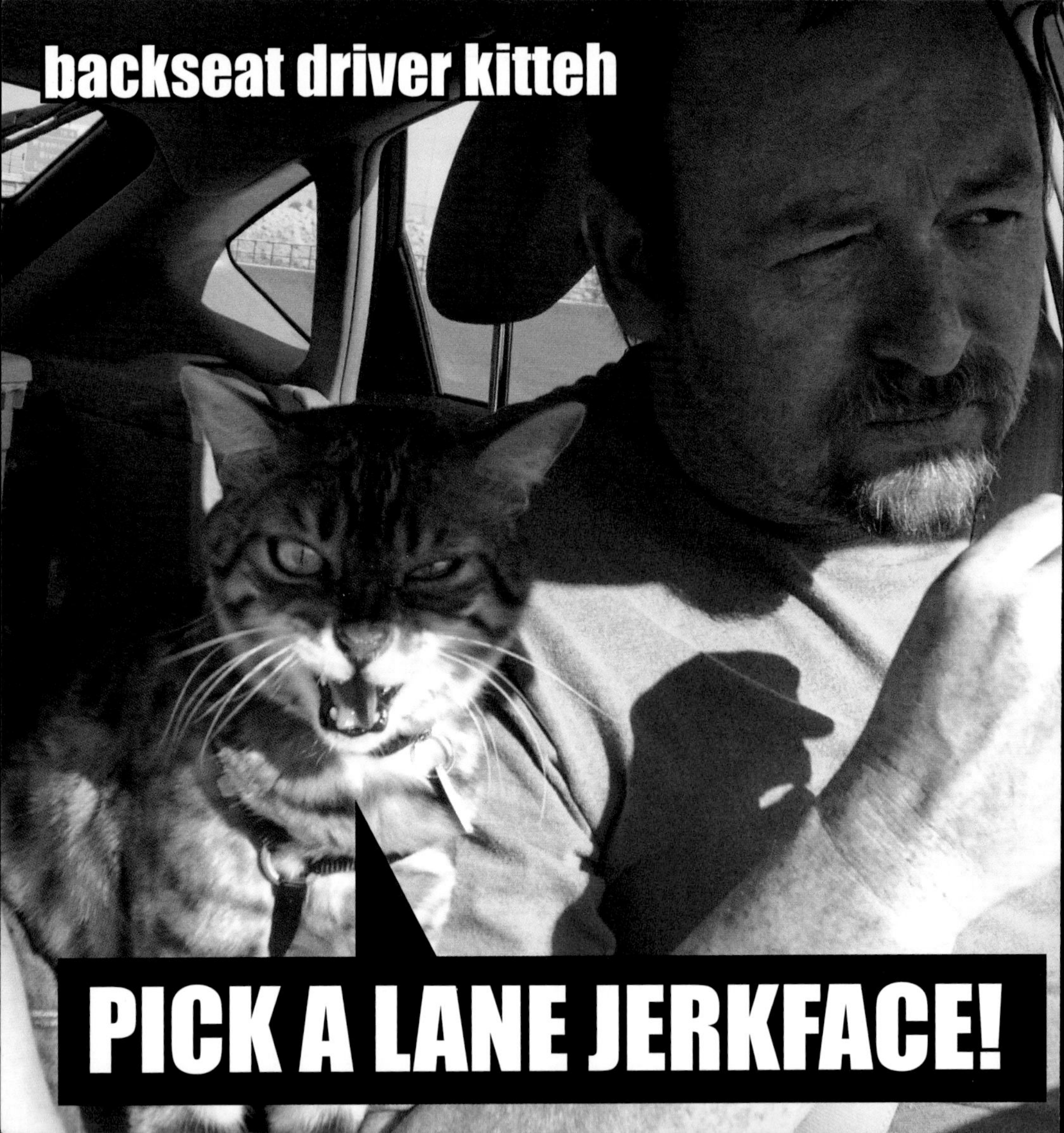
backseat driver kitteh
PICK A LANE JERKFACE!

Les try again frm 44.
Wach my tail dis time for accellerando ppl.
Nº 10. Sanctus.

OK, once again, 12345 is not a good password

Recipe for success

SHOULD

be here sumwhere...

Humans have no idea

how to properly use a basket.

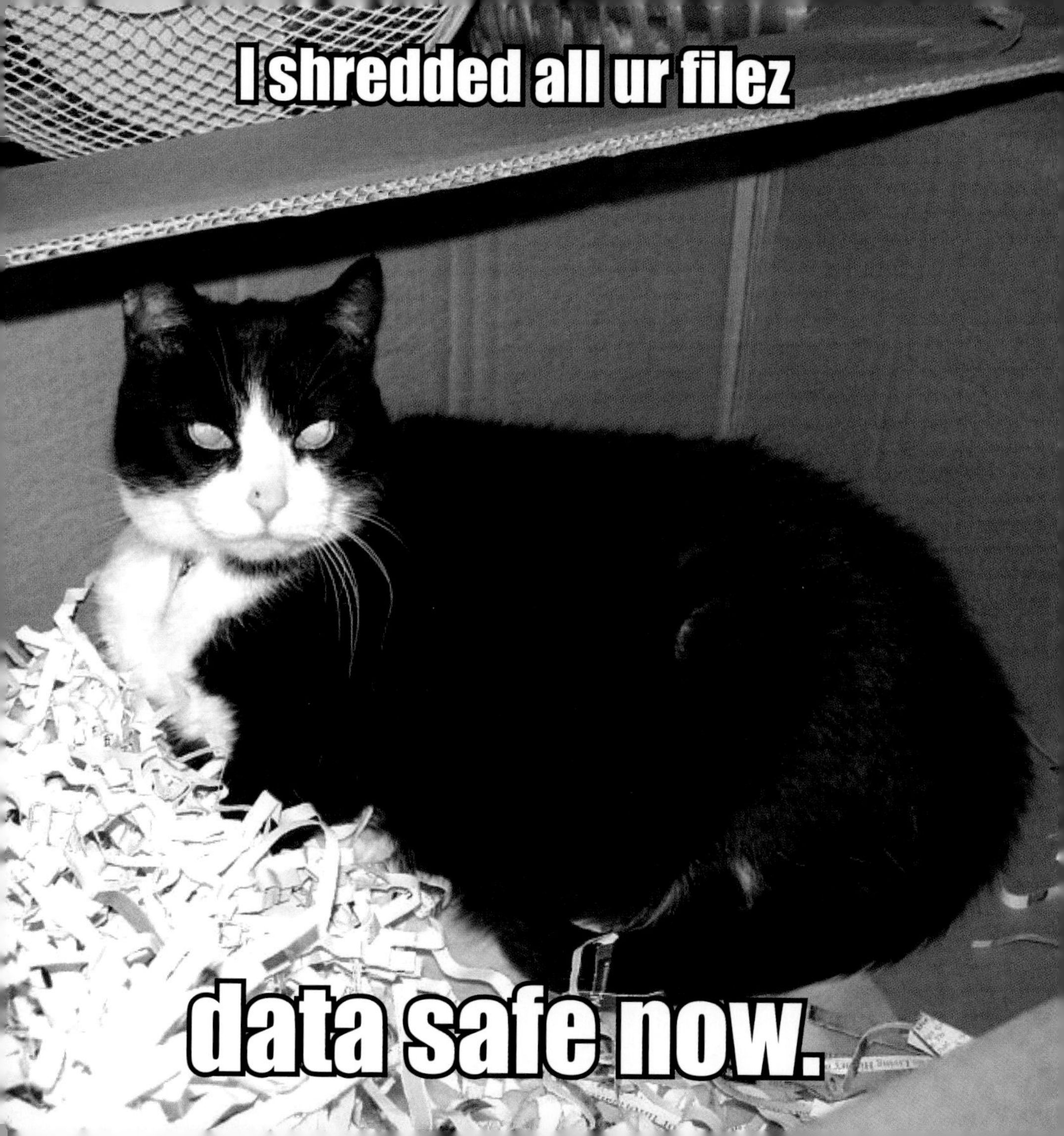
I shredded all ur filez
data safe now.

Hao much yoo pai for doze art lessuns?

Can yoo gets reefund?

nao,
abowt yor
employment
it appeers dat micdonuldz is hiring
...an they provide a family discownt

Well, if you had read the directions like I told you
then we wouldn't be in this mess now would we?

I put ded sqwerel in bag in case U want snak on plane.

Is whipped cream & shaved chocolate
Capuccino
just too much to expect from you?

Bring me a frooty drink.
...wif a bendy straww.

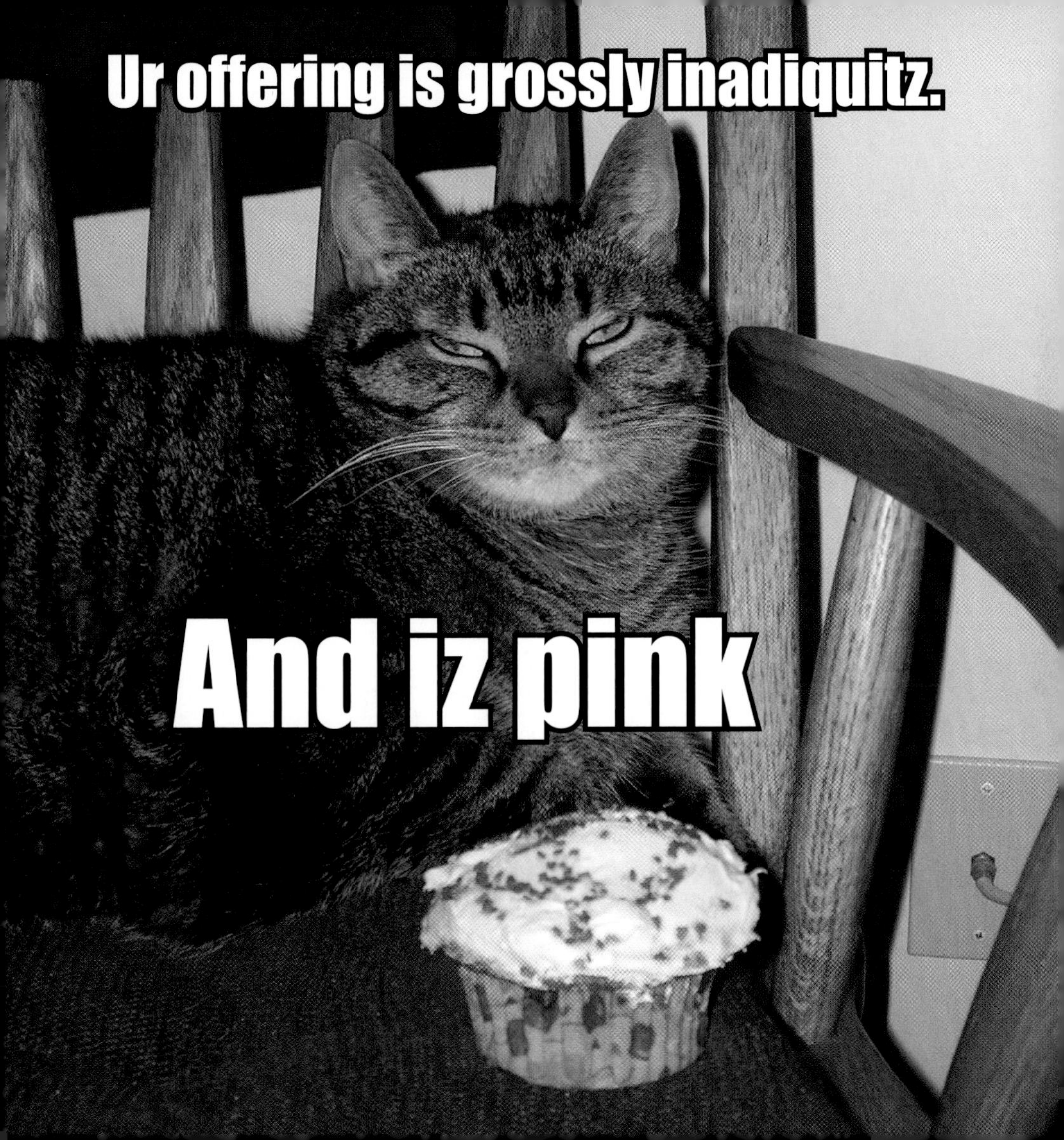
Ur offering is grossly inadiquitz.
And iz pink

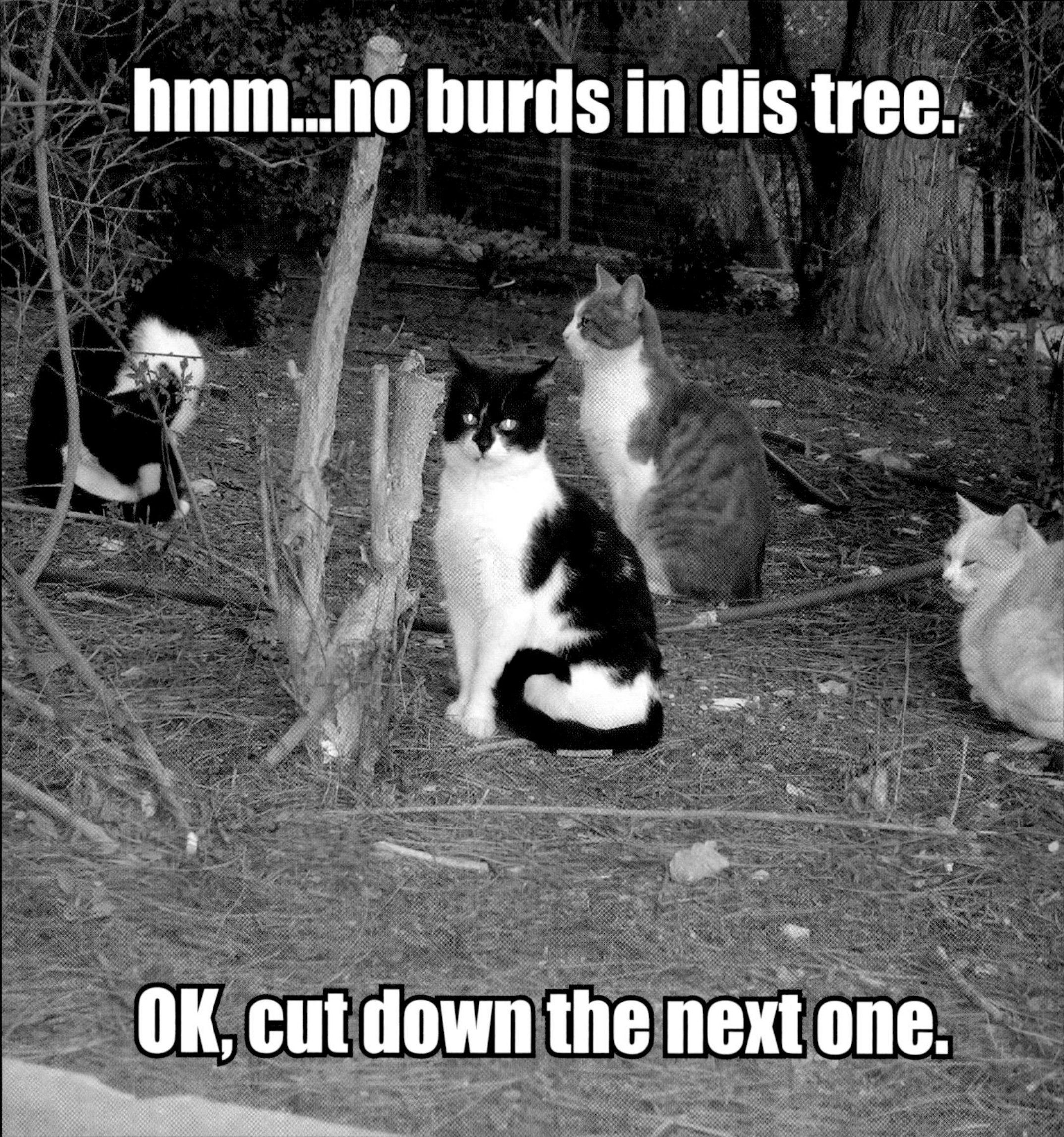
hmm...no burds in dis tree.
OK, cut down the next one.

Rock Climbing
the Wasatch

You apparently haven't heard the story of how my previous human died.

We reazonable zombys
Will take toona instead.
Iz totaly fine.

I ordered a latte
not a house blend

Sum sez haff full.
Sum sez haff emtee.
I sez haff MINE.
Uther haff mine too.

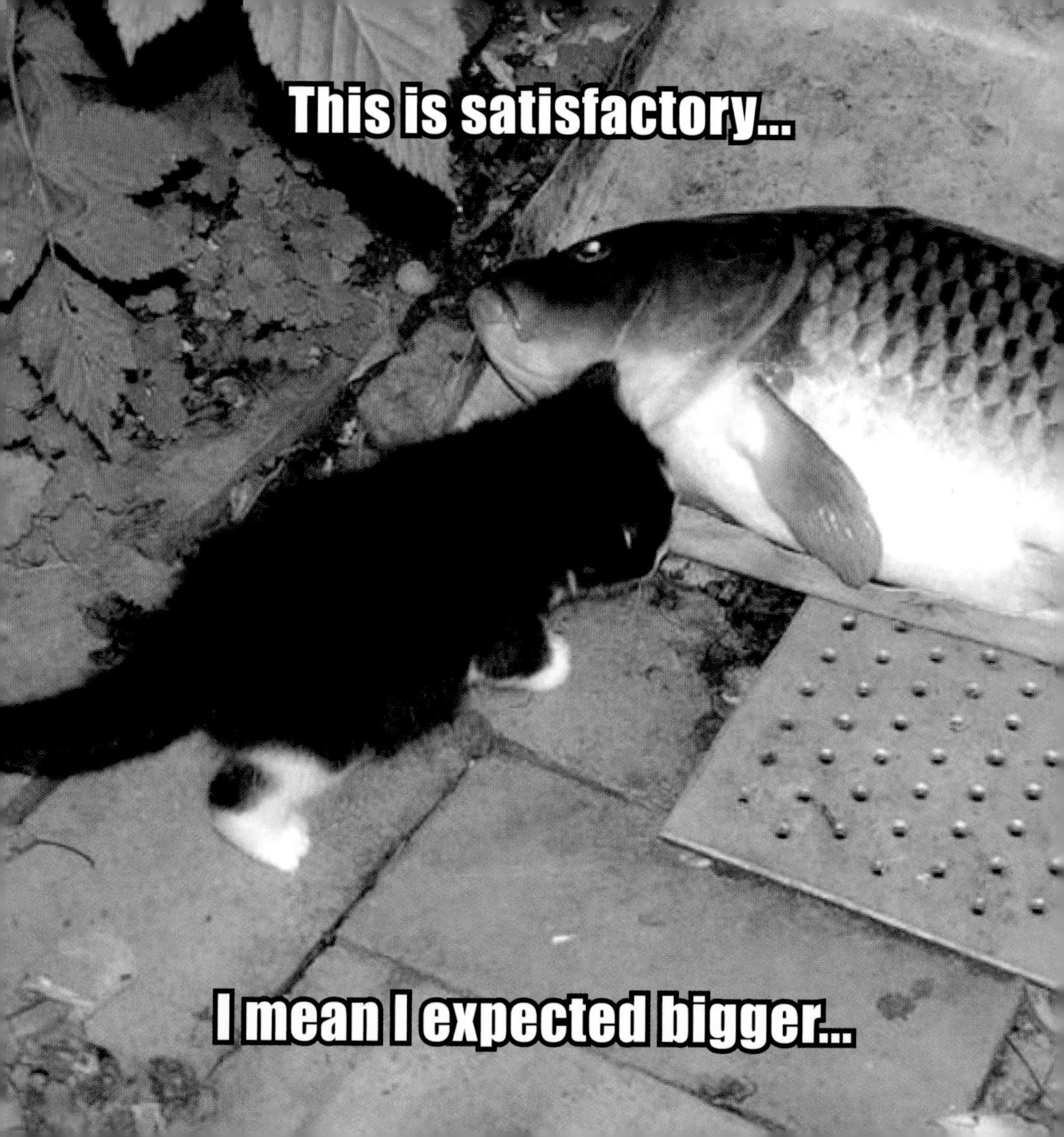
This is satisfactory...
I mean I expected bigger...

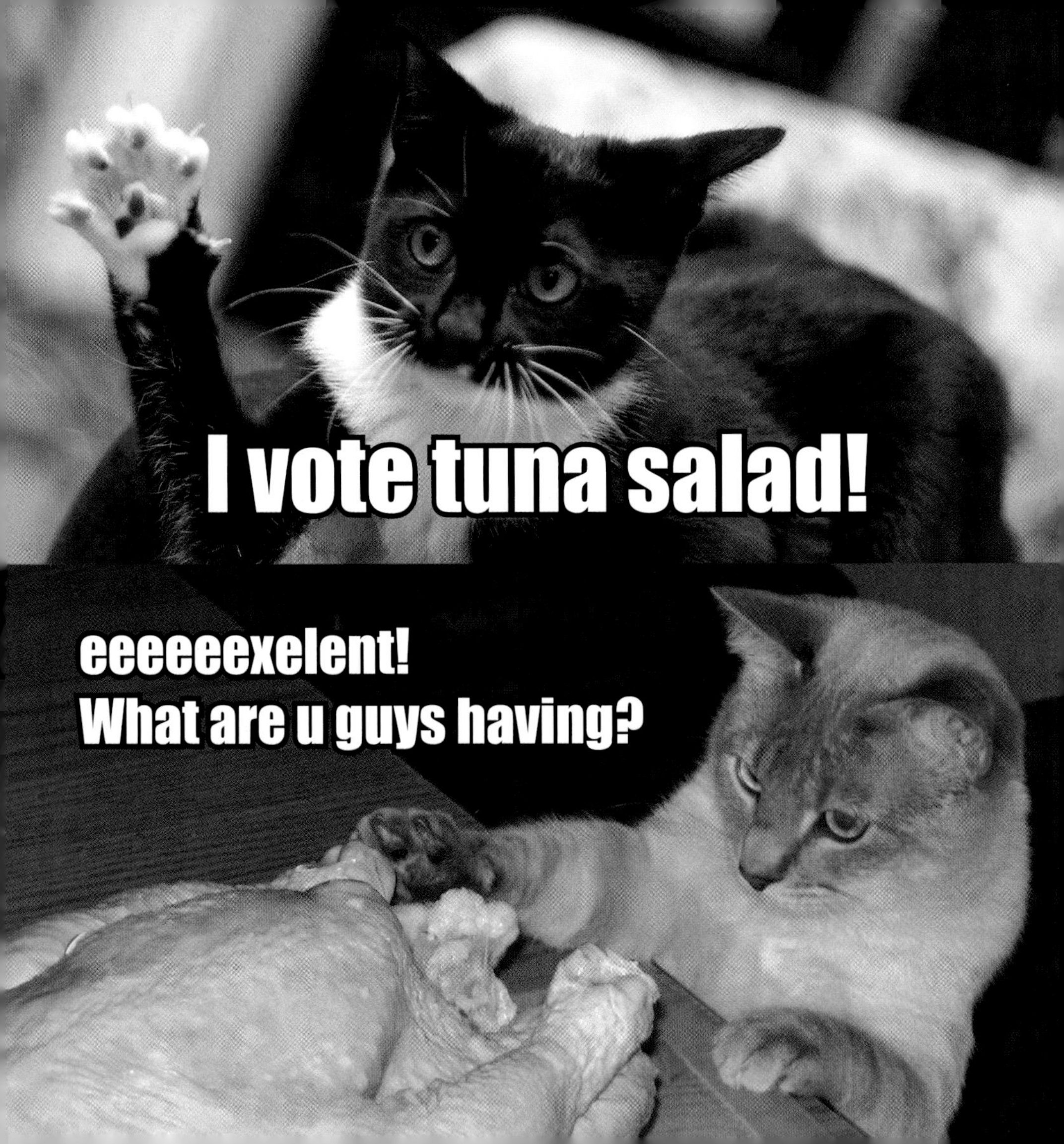
I vote tuna salad!
eeeeeexelent!
What are u guys having?

Hasnt u got enny noms dat nawt green?

I will be supervising your shopping trip
Makes shur you get the right cat treats this time.

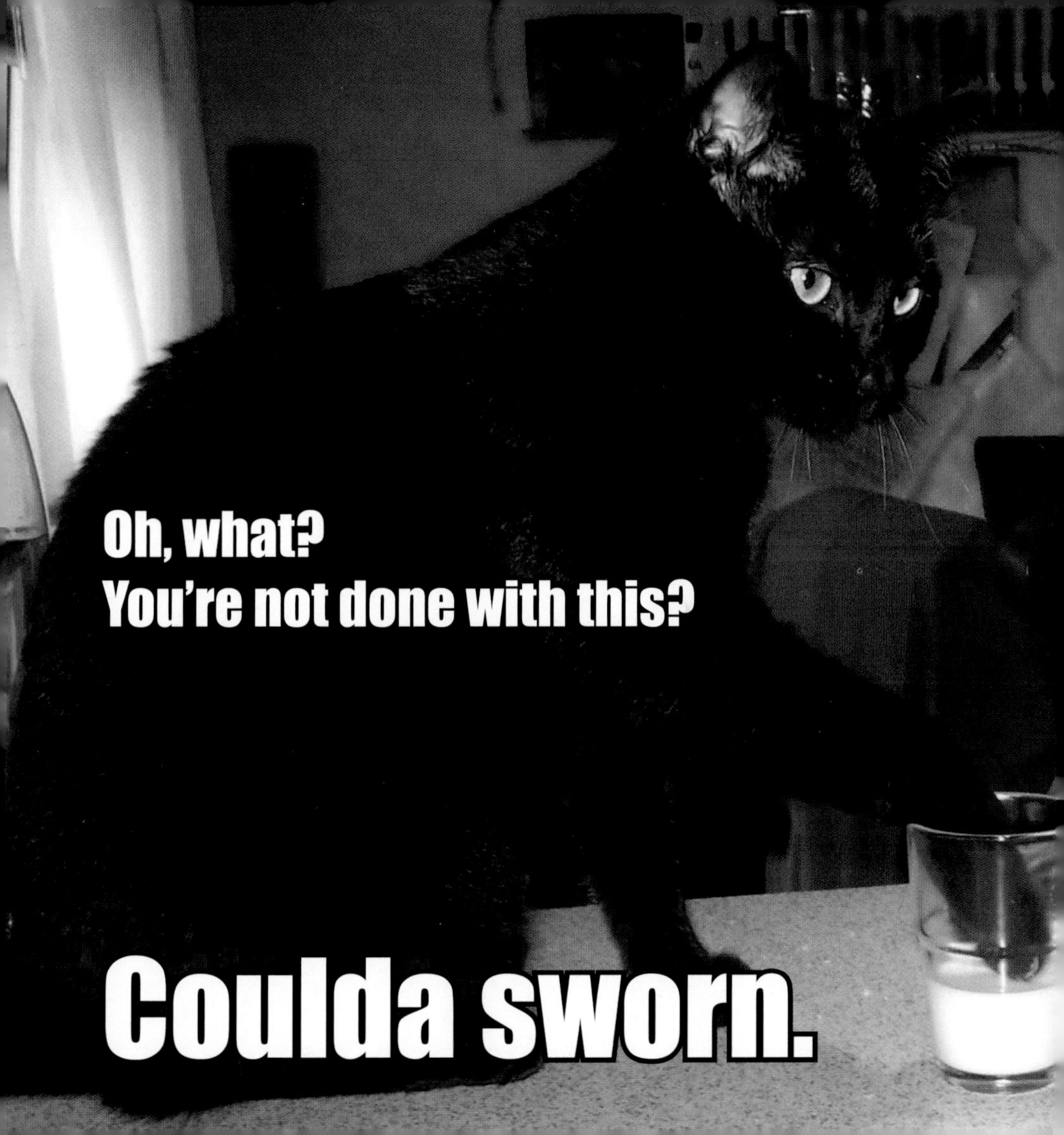
Oh, what?
You're not done with this?
Coulda sworn.

AROUND TEH HOUSE

You look upset. Did the children make another mess?

WHOAH! I have to admit ...
that is DEFINITELY a huge spider!
Okay, okay, calm down now ... and
bring me your shotgun.

Bob Vila cat sayz...

Applies the stain like dis...

You really need to clean my litter box more often.

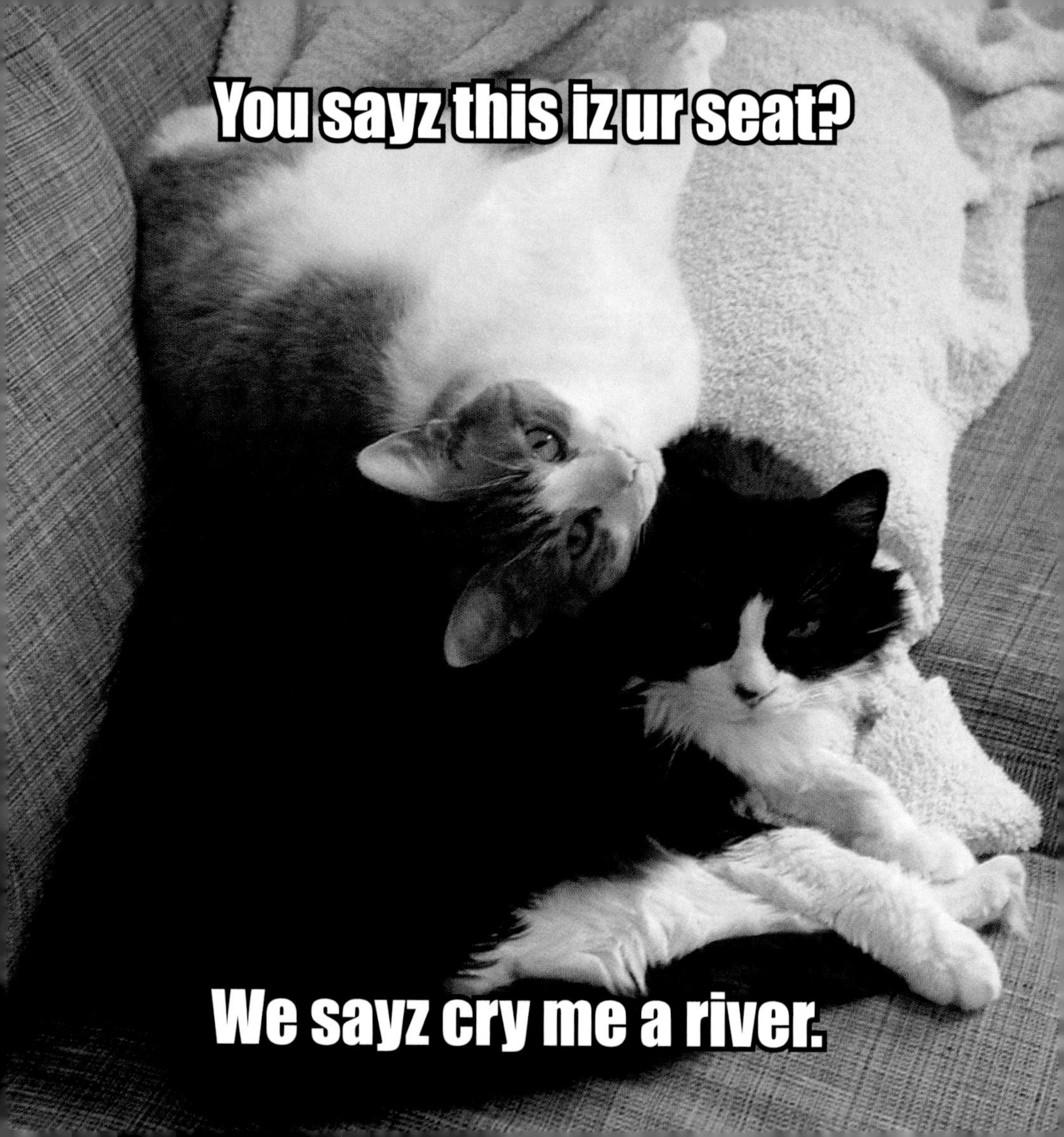
You sayz this iz ur seat?
We sayz cry me a river.

Whaddaya mean why dident ai tell u dey were towin ur car? AI DID!!!
Ai sed "meow mew meow meow meow" and u just looked at meh and smiled.

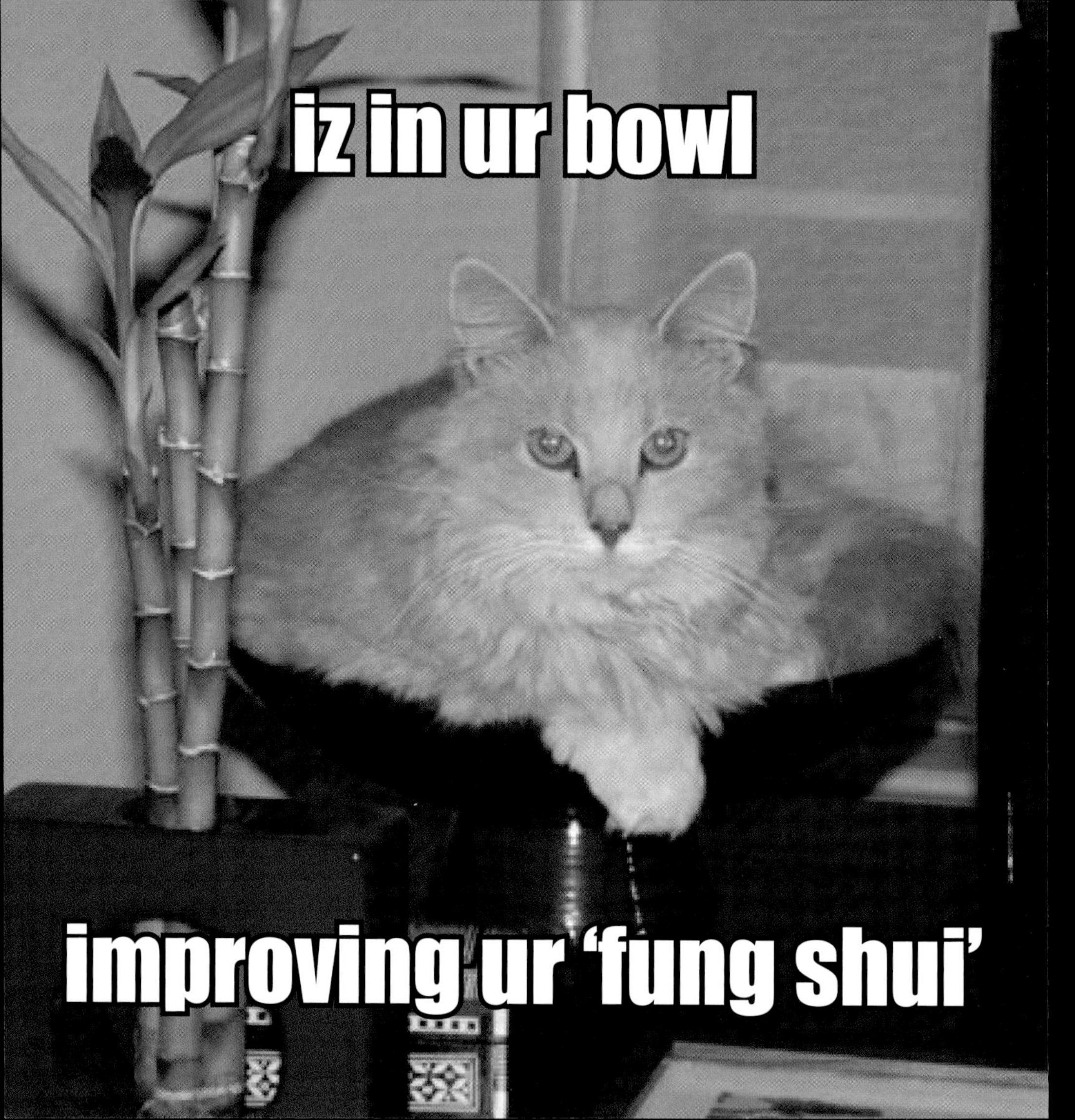
iz in ur bowl
improving ur 'fung shui'

one pillow for me

one pillow for tail

Um...we needz tu hab a tawk bowt yur howsekeepin habits.

Don't ask me! I cough it up,
you clean it up – that's the arrangement.

Why can't you ever talk about the times I DON'T destroy the toilet paper?! You never mention THOSE!

Dog was wet.
But iz ok, I takes care of it for you.

You can tell it's bad when the cat feels motivated to clean...

No. No more vacuum. Not ever.

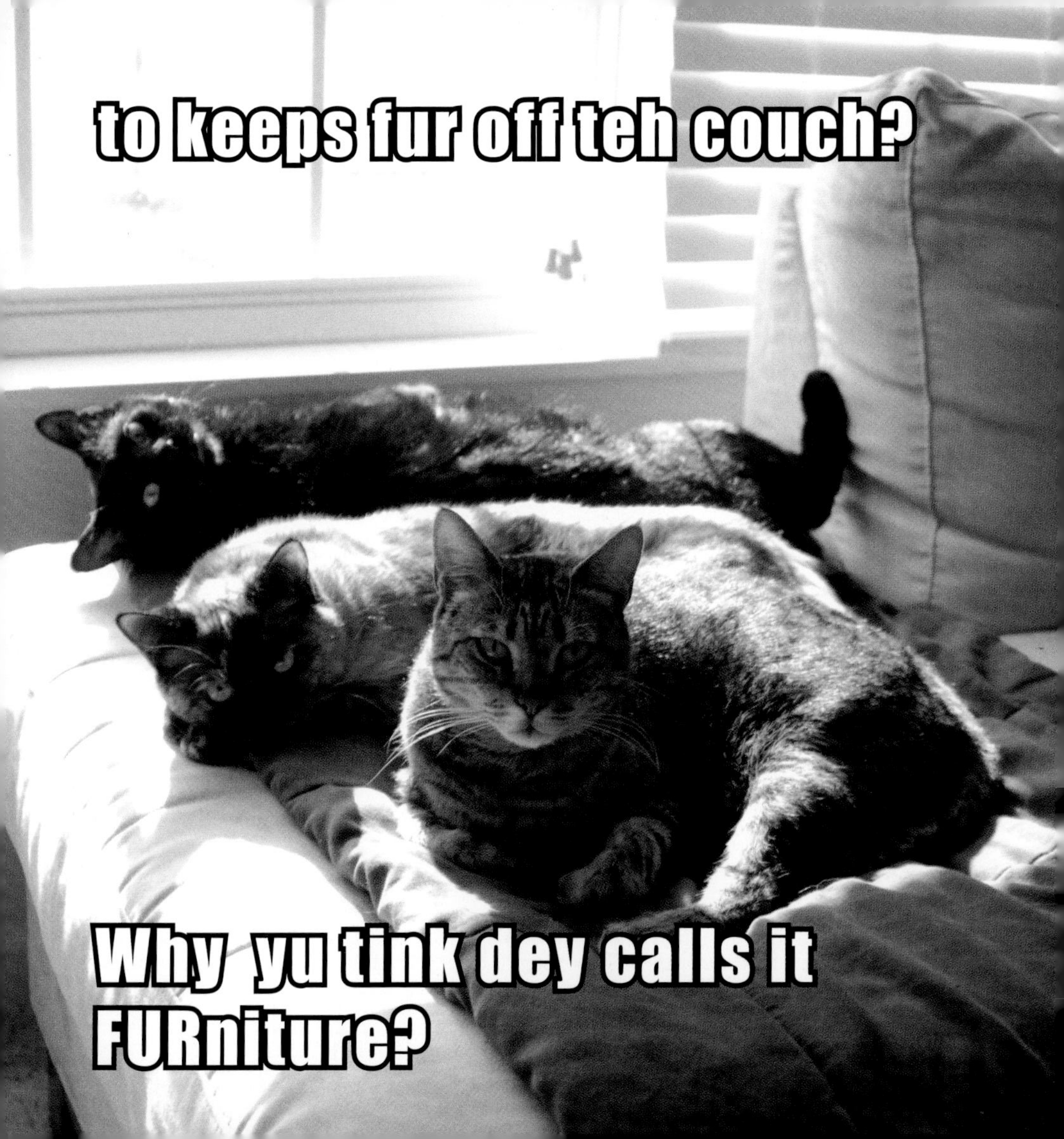
to keeps fur off teh couch?
Why yu tink dey calls it FURniture?

All dis plasticks gonna be nasty in teh summer. Jus sayin is all.

We would like to have a word with you about this new generic cat litter.

Lumbar kitteh

is being supportive

Crime scene sheets. Freaky.

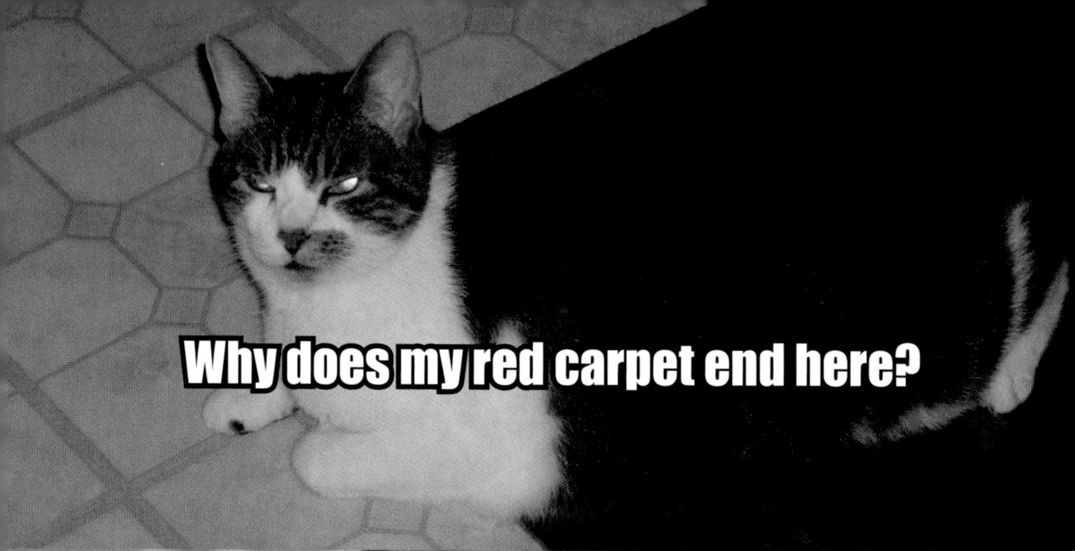
Why does my red carpet end here?

Set for Fluff Pleze
CLEAN BEFORE LOADING

Queschun iz

did change com to mai literbox?

Ugh. If you didn't buy such hideous upholstery, I wouldn't have to shred it.

Kitteh bed wit tail extenshun?
u finally did good hooman

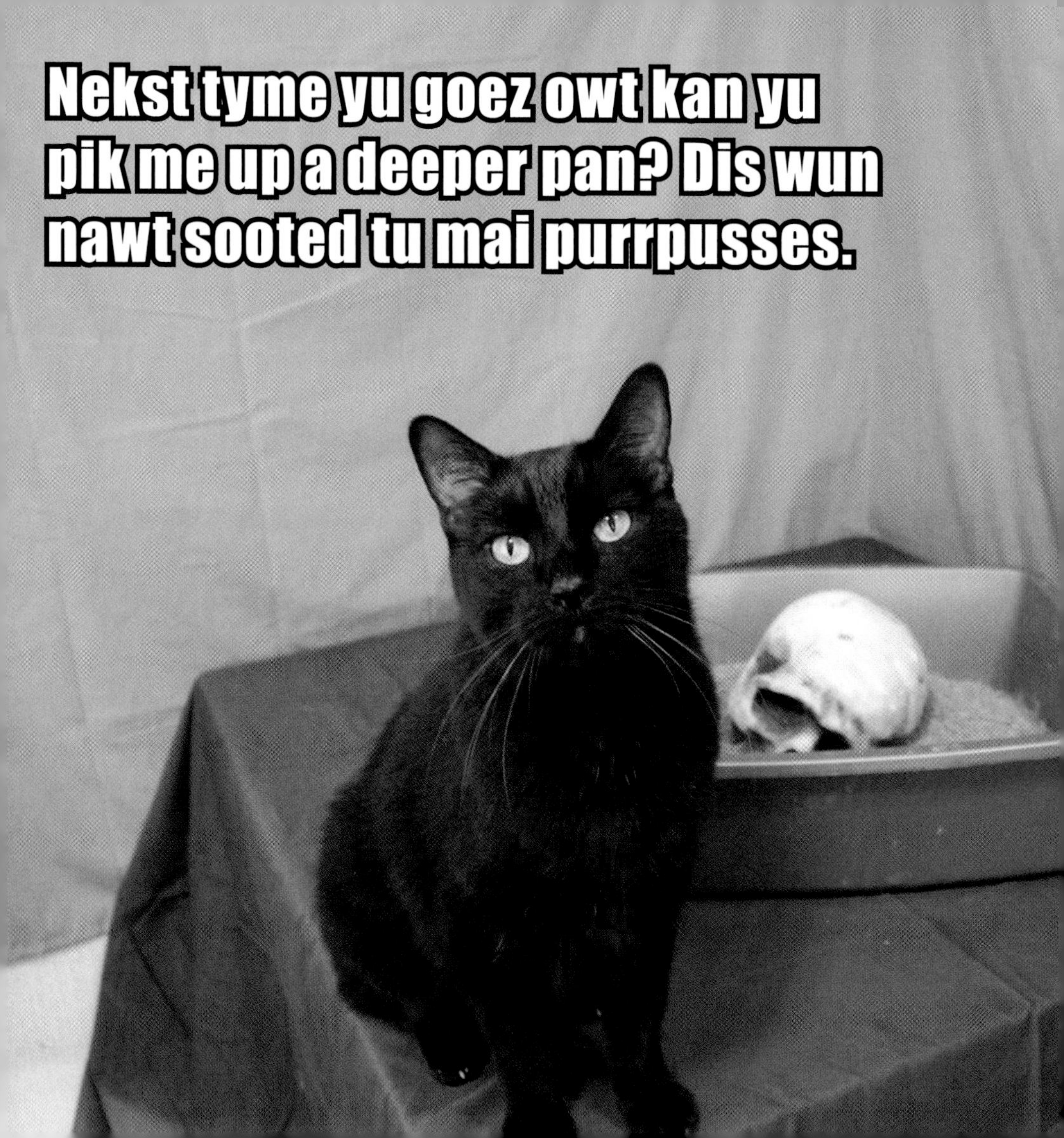
Nekst tyme yu goez owt kan yu pik me up a deeper pan? Dis wun nawt sooted tu mai purrpusses.

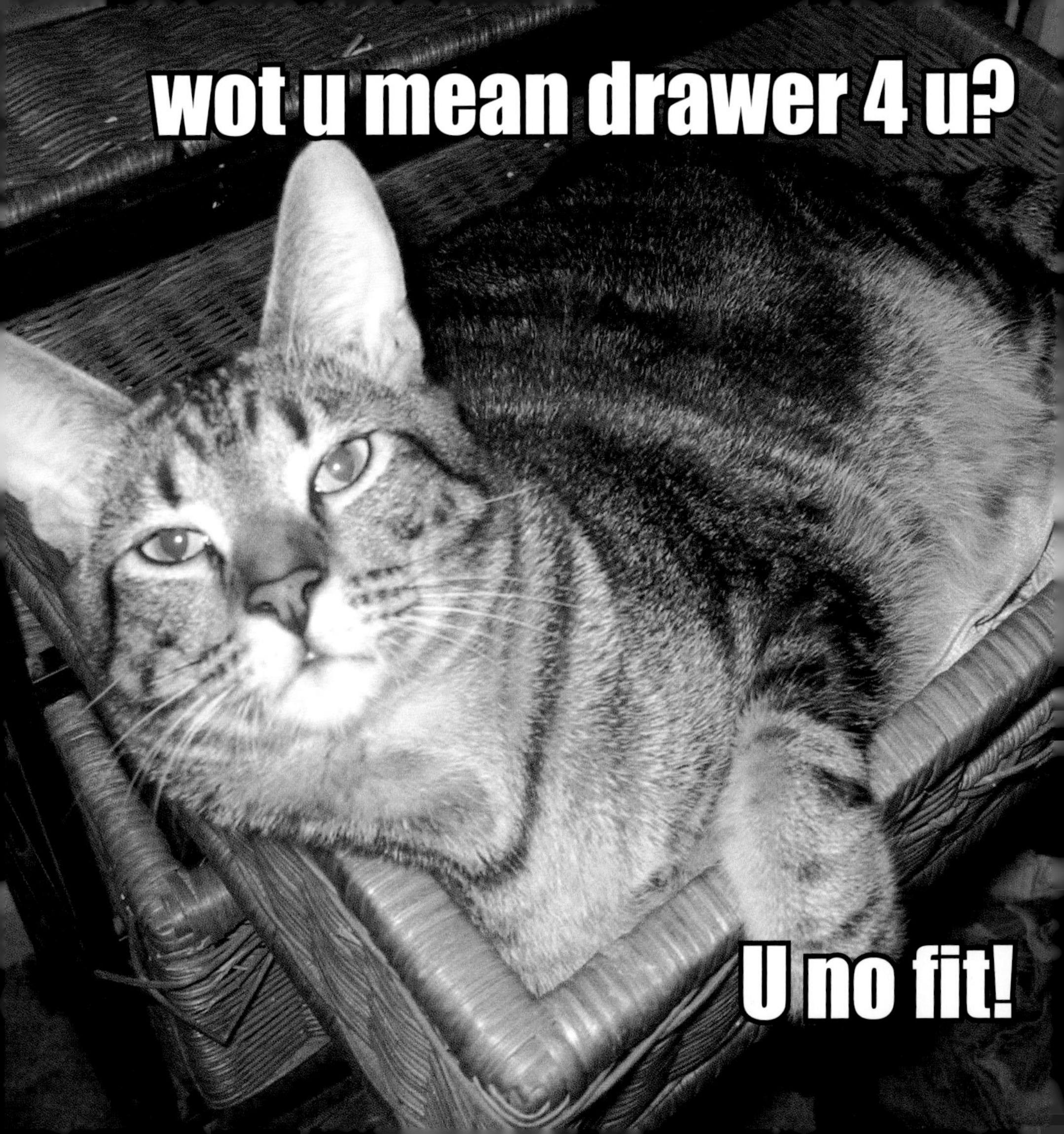
wot u mean drawer 4 u?
U no fit!

I'z on ur fork
helpin u keep ur rezolooshuns.

Don't hate me cuz I bootfyful
Hate me cuz I throwd up on ur bed

You certainly have a lot of beauty products for someone of your...

appearance.

Thank Gawd teh odder bridezmaidz also stuk wearin teh same lilac loser dress.

Kitteh fashul: furst wi exfoiliate an din follow up wit a gud toner.

We'll lick ur pore problum in no tiem.

You aksually wear dis?

To join me for tea you must change out of those jeans.

Iz not bosseh

I jus noe whut u shudz b doin

SILENCE!
If I want your opinion, I'll give it to ya!
Now hush, or I'll bop ya on the noggin.

Hoomin? Why have you closed that door? You know very well that you're not supposed to close any doors in my house. Unless of course it is to keep the dog outside. But I don't hear any whining on the other side of this door, so this is clearly a case of unauthorized door-closing on your part. You will rectify this situation immediately.

Your cat goddess awaits her sacrifice--
the dog and gerbil should do nicely

Diet Kitteh...
silently judges you

But I've played with these once,

I need NEW toys.

Okai, we can do dis one ov two wayz.
MY way, or da scratchey, bleedy,
use-up-all-da-band-aidz way.
I lets U chooz cause either wai iz cool wif me.

silence hooman

iz tired of ur voice

Will you watch what you're doing
next time you slam a door?
There could be people behind it,
you know, trying to sleep!

Amish cat does not approve of your fancy washing machine

come wit me stupid human

Toylit Kitteh
Maekin Shur yew wipe AND flush

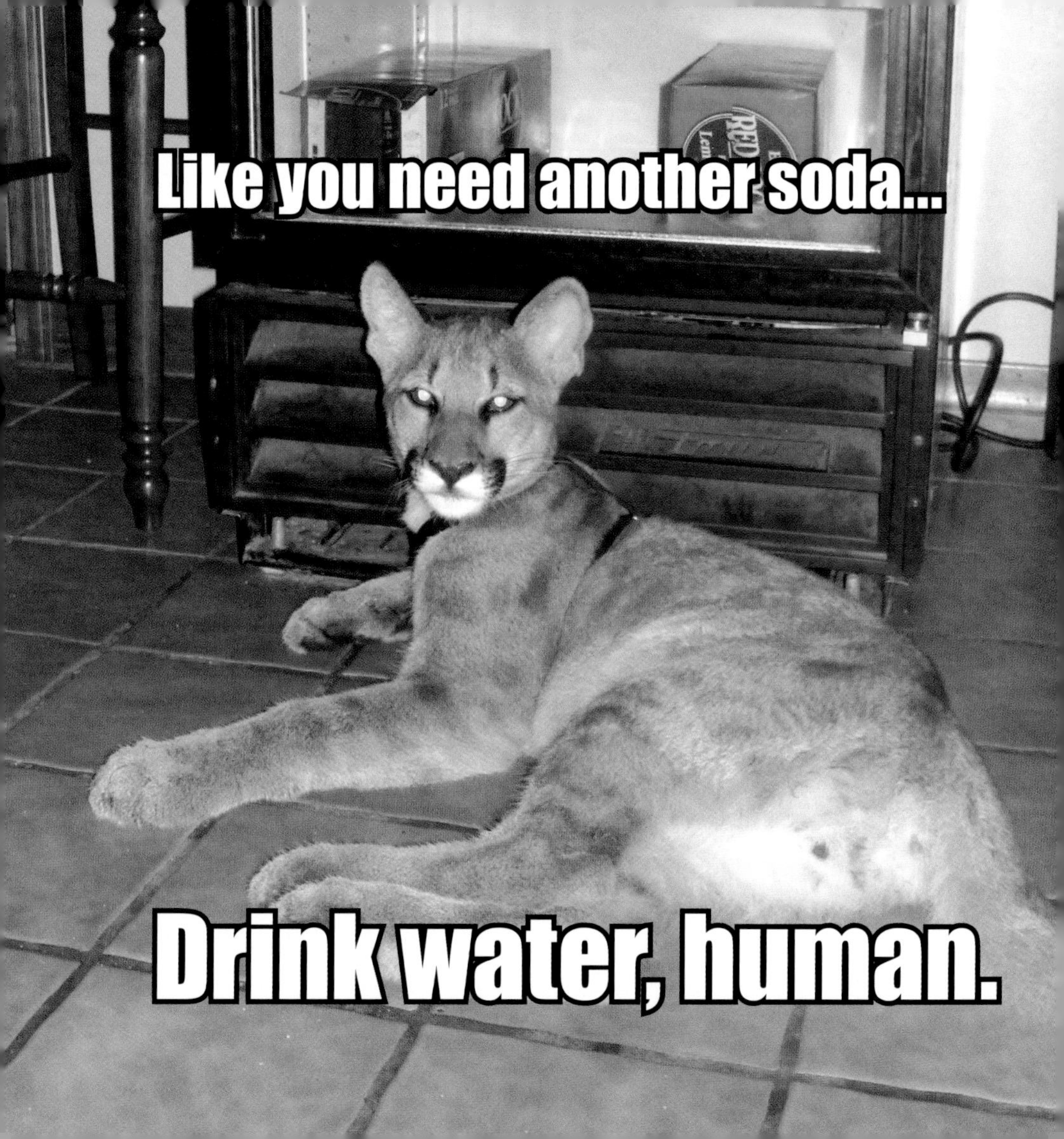
Like you need another soda...
Drink water, human.

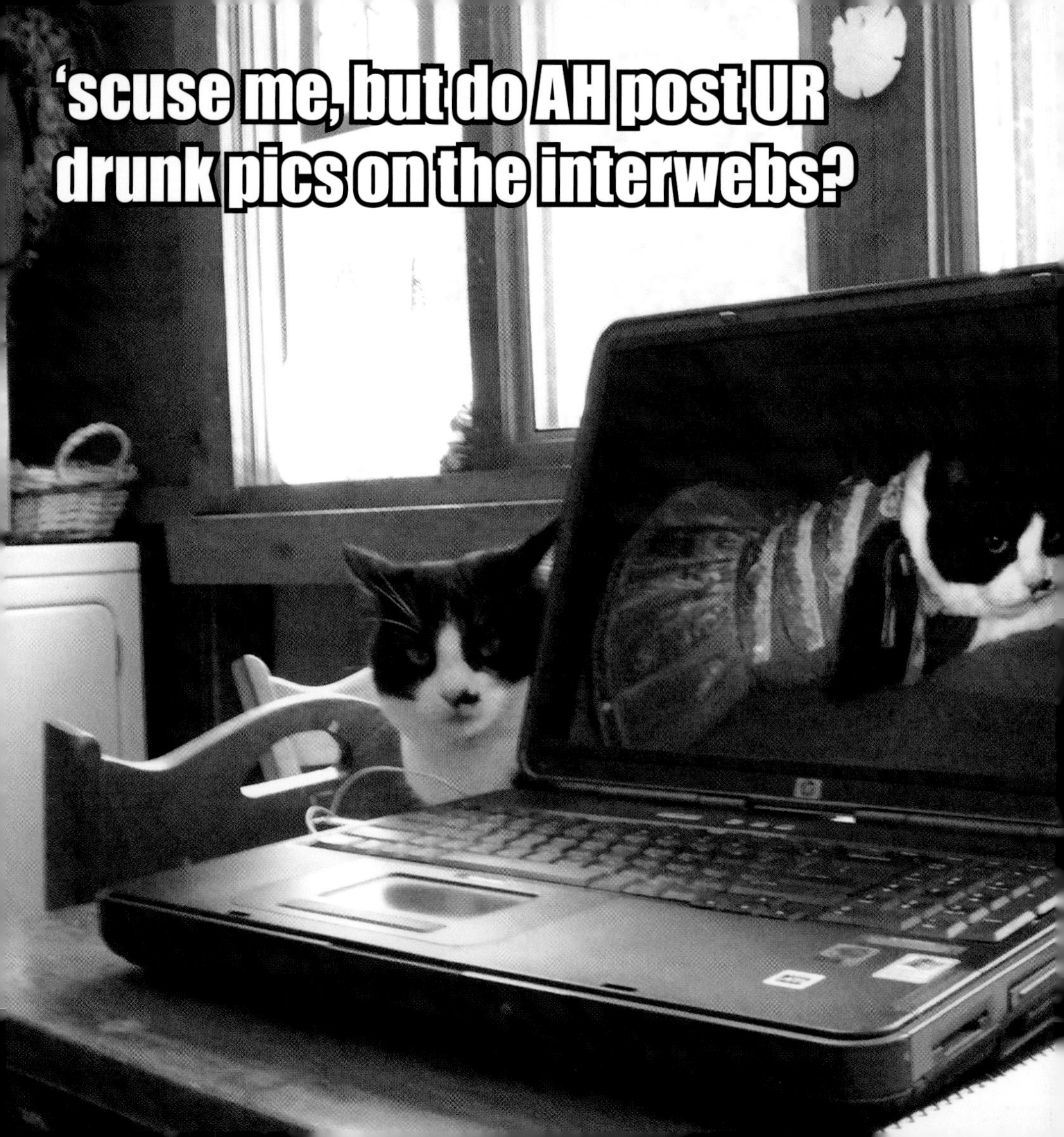
‘scuse me, but do AH post UR
drunk pics on the interwebs?

Hullo...I iz ur nu AA sponsor...
Go ahed, reach 4 ber...

Yu read dis one...

Kittens FOR **DUMMIES**

Den go back to da bookstore and getz me a copy of "Dummies for Kittens" so eberybuddy will be up to speed, k?

A Reference

DIS YER NEW SKEDULE. PINK MEANZ YU FEEDZ MEH, 'N GREEN ONEZ ARE CHOREZ: CLEAN'N' LITTERBOX, PETTIN' ME 'N STUUFFZ LIK DAT

If you insist on surfing the internet before feeding me, might I suggest you Google "scars and lacerations, emergency treatment."

Study? Wut u meen study?
U pay attenshun to only meh.
Its the rules.
No study.

Bridezilla cat
wants alternations done

NAO!

OH NOES – TEH NEKKID YOGA AGIN.

I am more important than anything that happens in your human world anyway.

Dumbledore dies

nao feedz me!

Ya know, if we could just agree on this "no baths" thing you'd be able to take the paramedics off speed dial.

U stop playin now
Is food and hugs tiem.

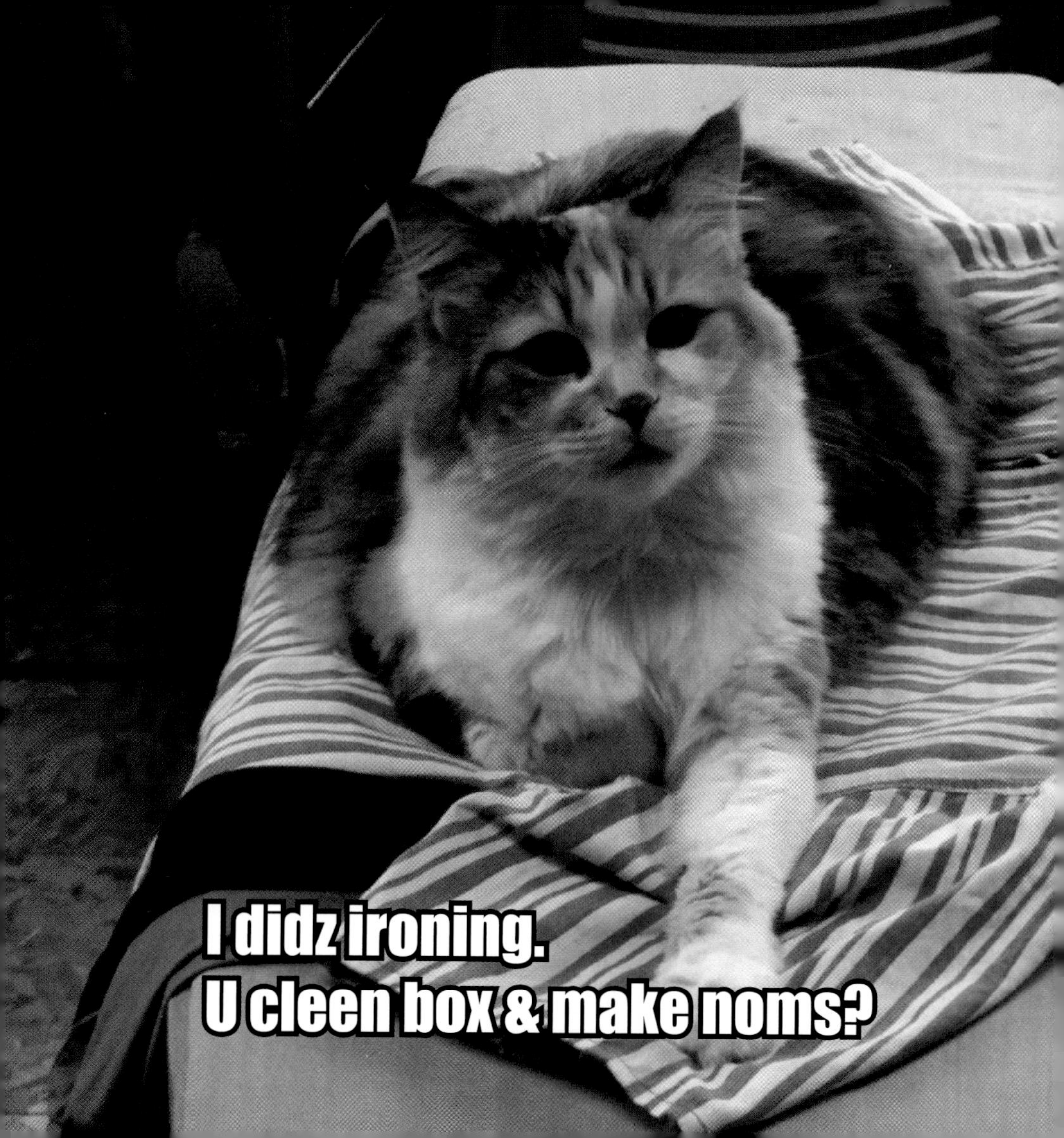
I didz ironing.
U cleen box & make noms?

unhealthy interests

u has them.

ne of Tyrants

orizon

Hitler—In 1923 a German war
to satisfy his hunger for re-
lief, attempted to overthrow
ment in Munich. The failed
ler in jail, which gave him
on his personal memoir of
Struggle), In a rambling
forth his ideas for a new
and scrapping the League
many of the "weakening"
uniting all Germans, and
als and Jews. After his
his doctrines to growing
Hitler and his National

Thank you for covering me up but now if you could turn off the light and sing to me.

Ai halps wif ur projekt
knit 1, purrl 1, nom awl teh rests!

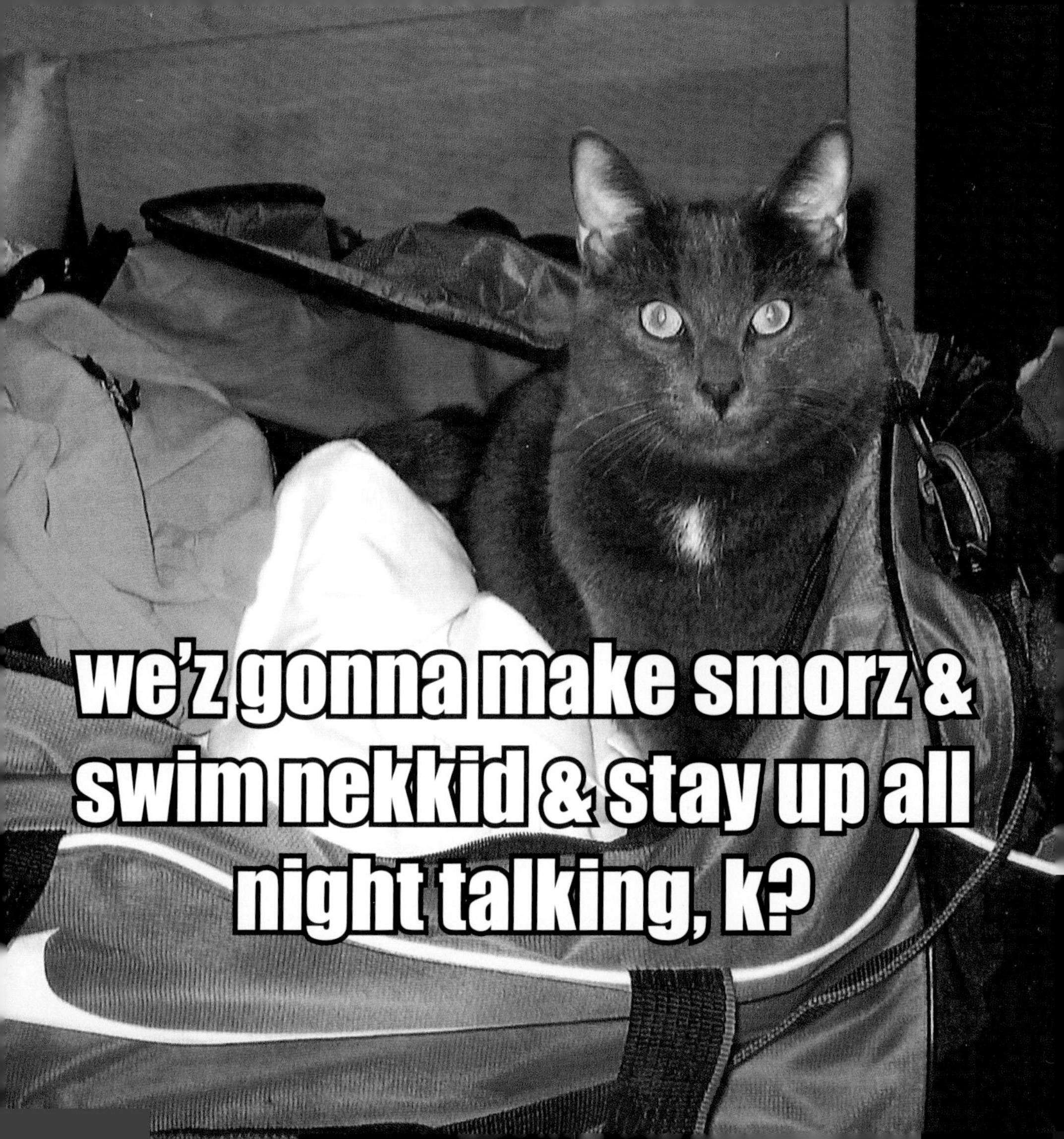
we'z gonna make smorz &
swim nekkid & stay up all
night talking, k?

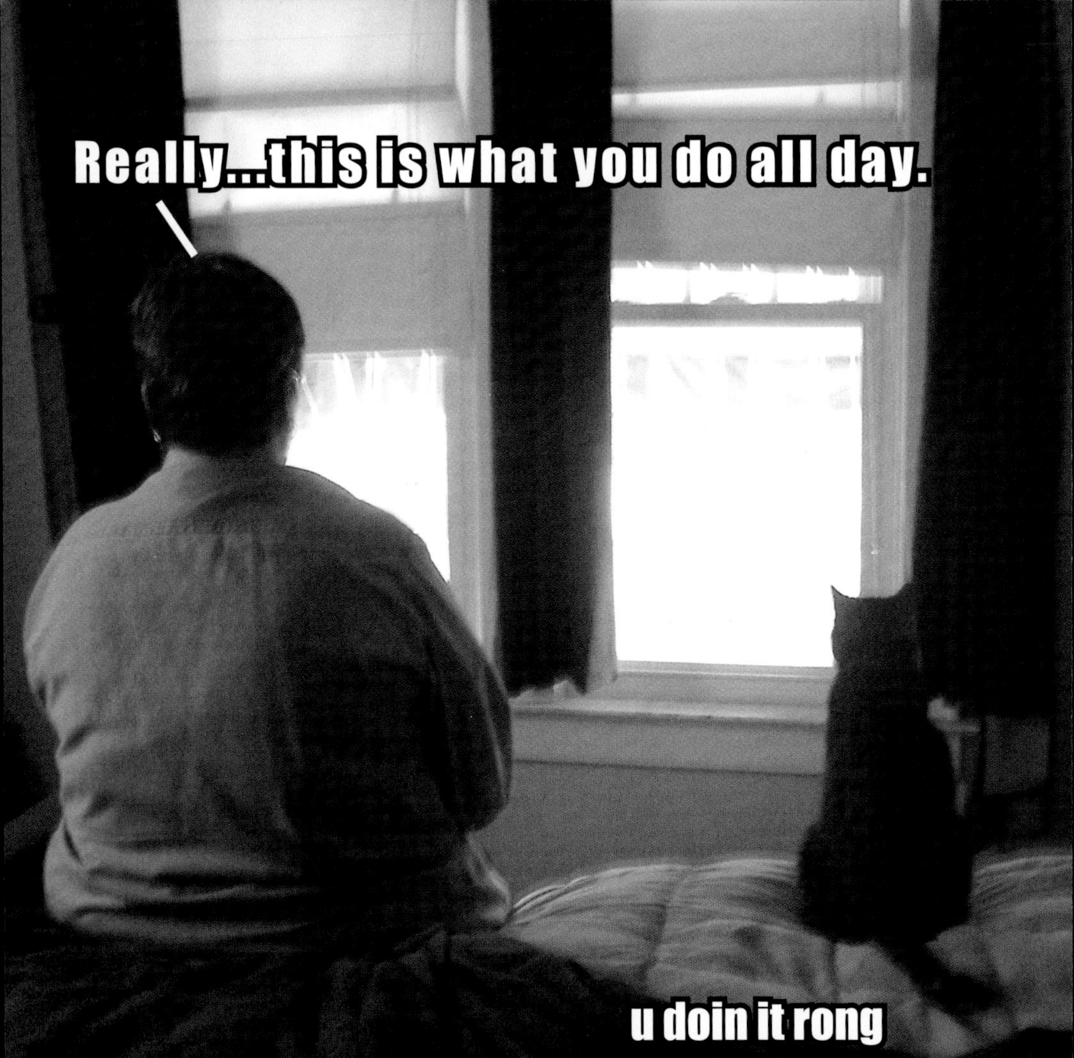
Really....this is what you do all day.
u doin it rong

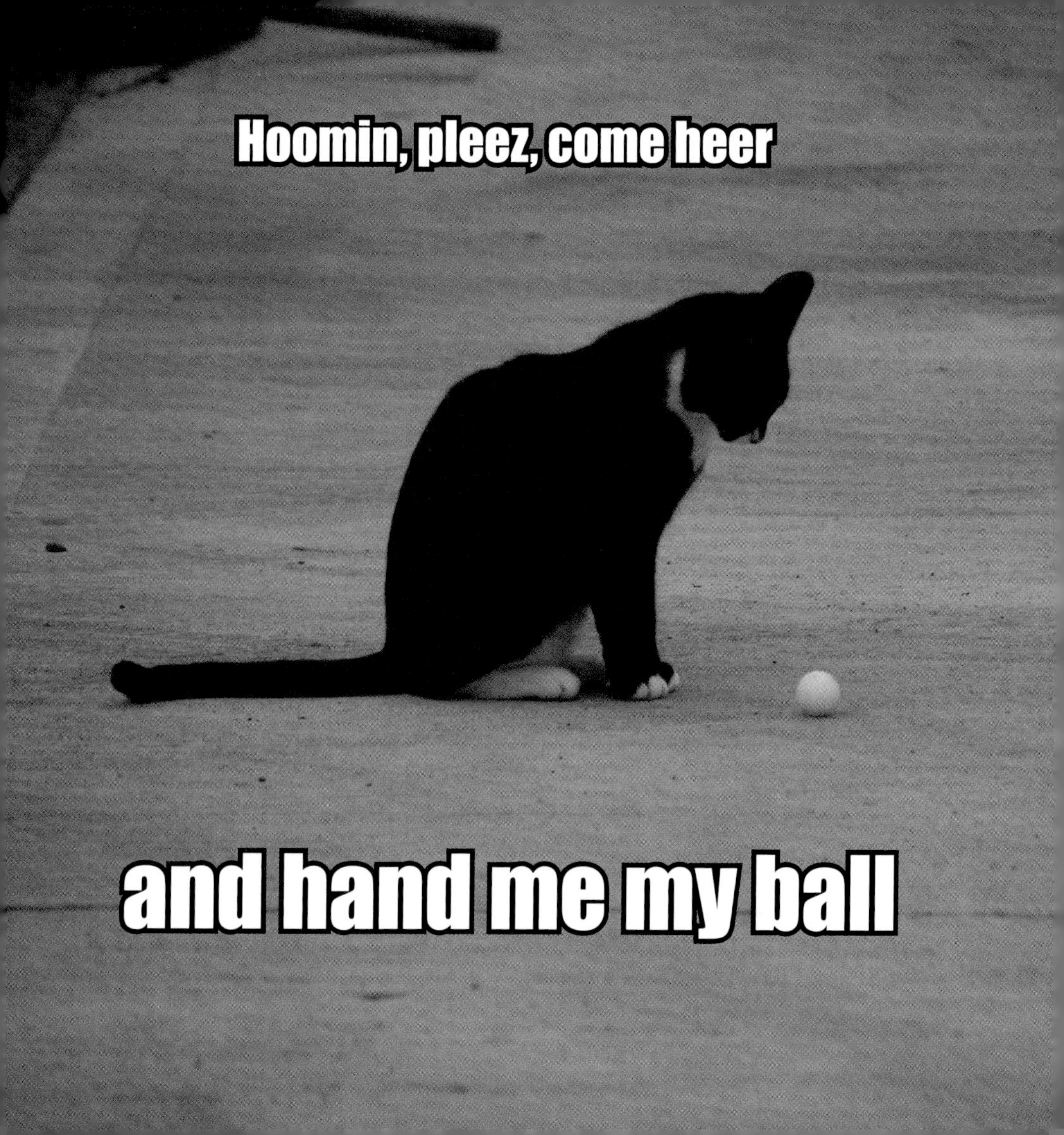
Hoomin, pleez, come heer
and hand me my ball

K, I beleeves I haz FINALLY had nuff petting.
Yuz kin stopz now. . . . hello?

Yep. As usual, you're doing diddly squat.

Why iz I not part of your planz today?

I get to be the shoe, or NOBODY plays

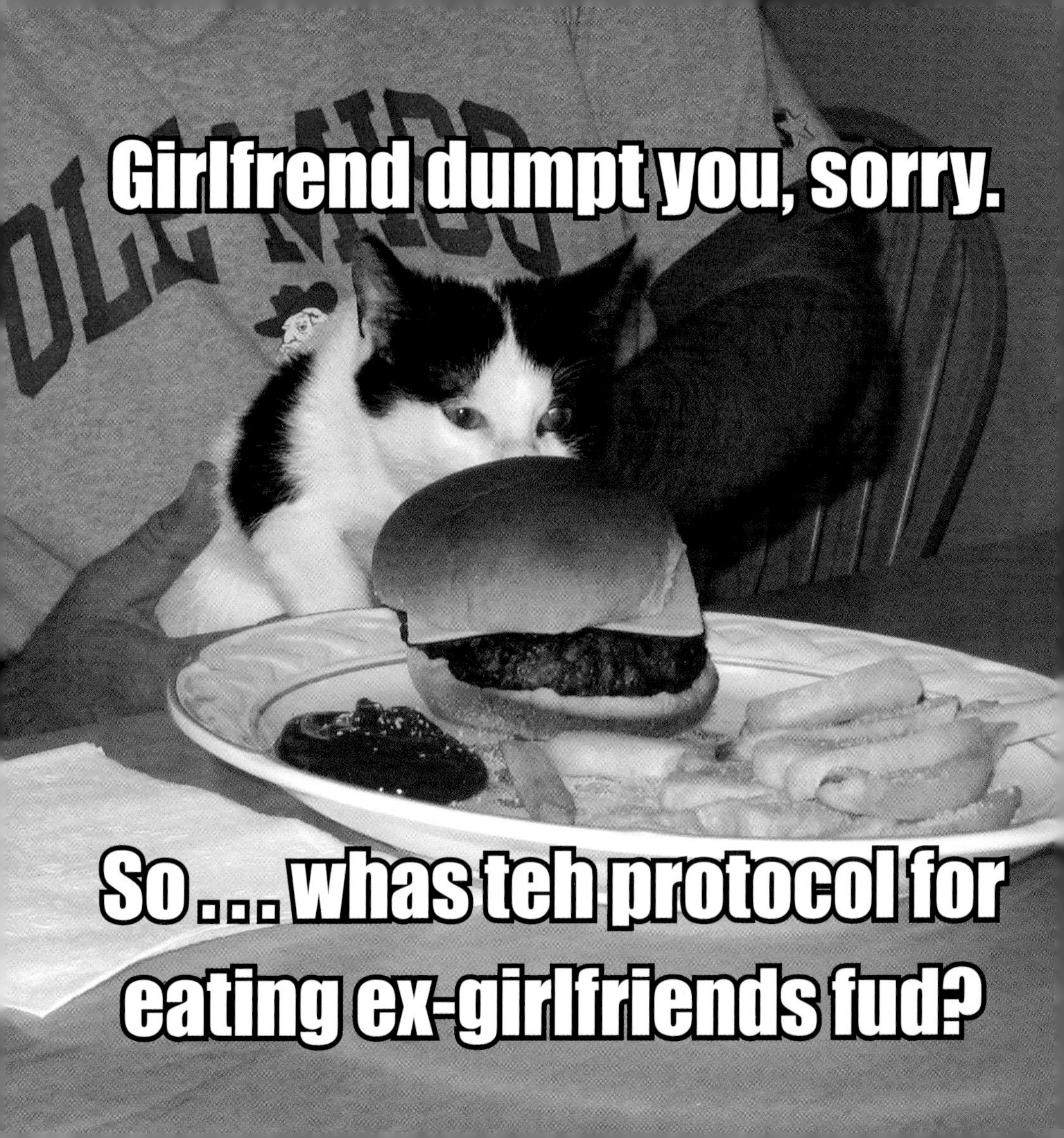
Girlfrend dumpt you, sorry.
So . . . whas teh protocol for
eating ex-girlfriends fud?

Chastity Cat
ish protecting your
daughters
Could be worse...
You culd haz a boyfrind or a
huzband or sumfin!

Don't give meh that "cootchy coo" crap—

YOU'RE LATE WITH MY NOMS!

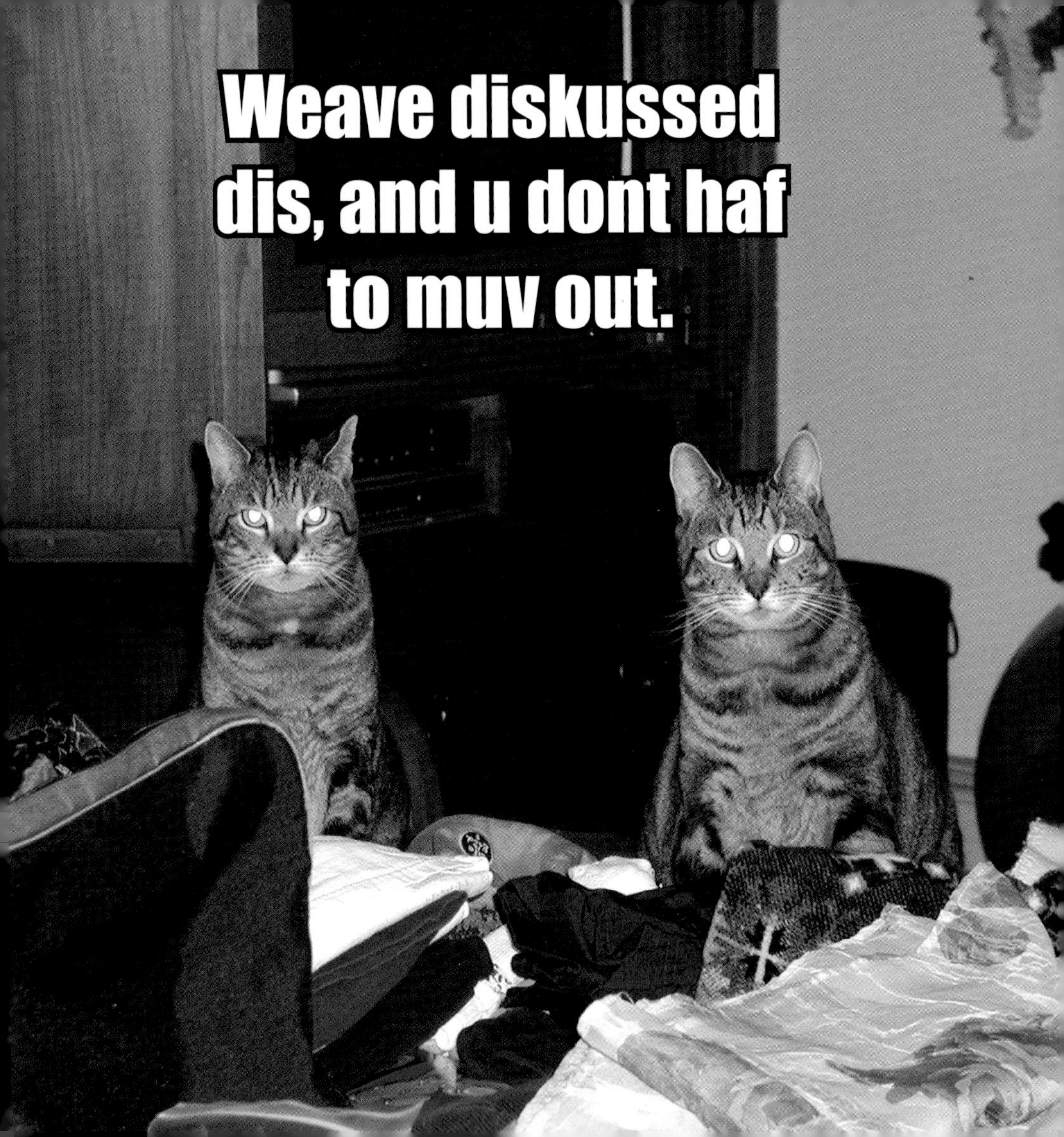
Weave diskussed
dis, and u dont haf
to muv out.

Iz never havin kids
theyz poopin, theyz cryin.....
theyz hasselin the kitteh...

Yeah, I'm really sorry that loser left ya...
but u cudda least saved me a taste a this.

.... now please allow me to bite a mouse in half and smoosh it against your lips.

I did the Math

we can't afford the Dog

kitteh heers your cries for help
n kitteh is indifferent to them

DON'T LET THIS HAPPEN TO YOU!
Please have your human
spayed or neutered.

Haven't you done enough already?

Up Close & Purrsonal

I like yu.

Yur nawt veree brite, but yu tryz hard.
Nao go fech me sum toona.

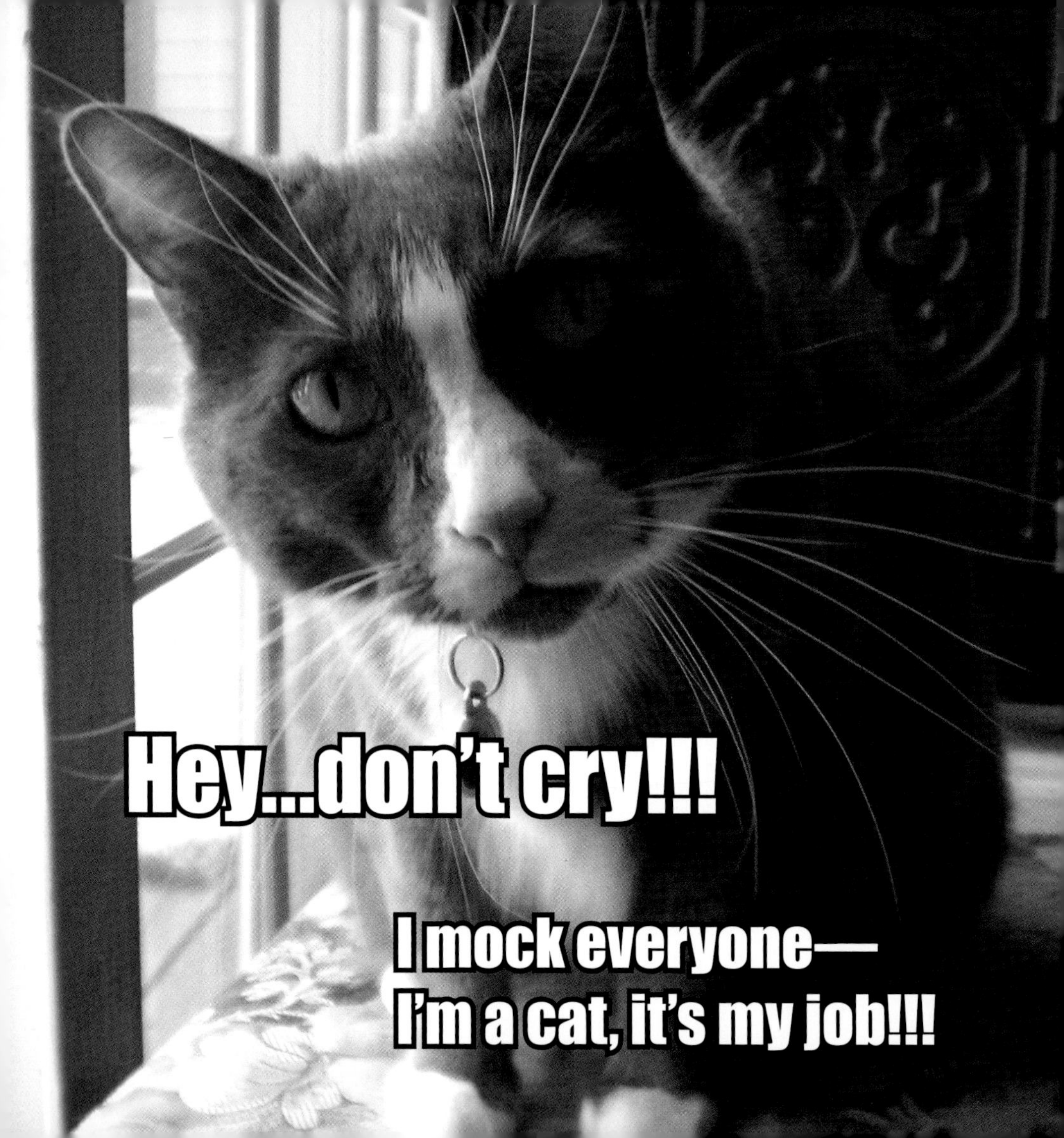
Hey...don't cry!!!
I mock everyone—
I'm a cat, it's my job!!!

share cheezburger
or face continued stink-eye

The next time you feel like "bonding," superglue yourself to the wall.

annoying neighbor kitteh

Ur yard haz weedz, Ur musik iz too loud, an Ur dog poopz in my yard!

You iz awake?

I need nomz.

You really need to learn to pace your naps, like I do. Just last week alone, you missed our 3am playtime twice and would have slept through Sunday if I hadn't pounced on your face.

Um, yu do kno dat depweshun is
jist anger wifowt enfuziazm, rite?

Dis wat u look like after party.

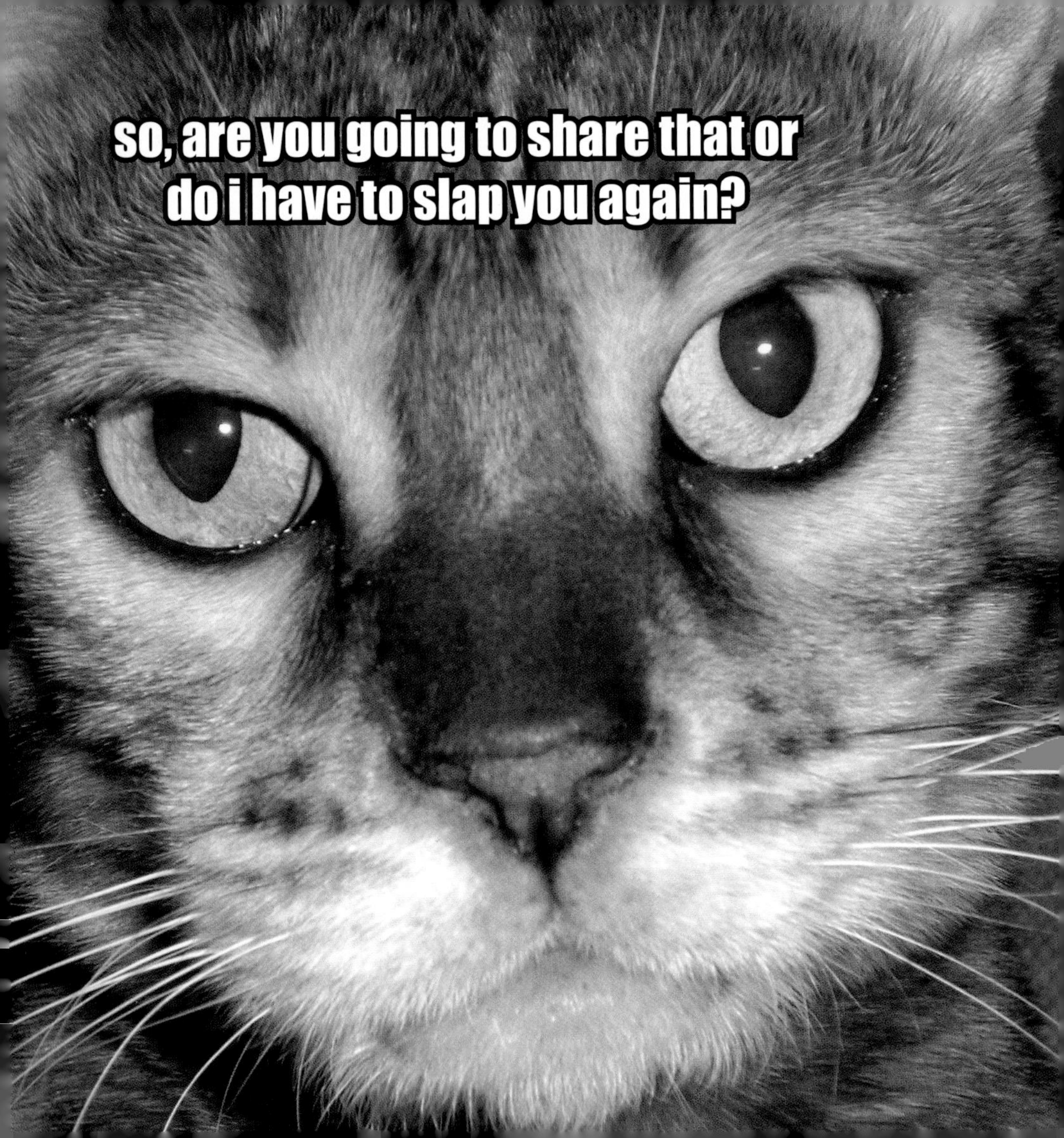
so, are you going to share that or
do i have to slap you again?

Liv evry day az if yu will die tumorrow

Cuz it kan be arranjed

CREDITS

Sonya Vatomsky, Todd Sawicki & Ben Huh: Editing

Joe Rufa: Chapter illustrations

Kittehs: Lookin' gud!

Thx to:

Matt Russoniello,
Matthew Martell,
Zach Hansen,
Nick "Big Cat" Mangione
& the rest of the team at Cheezburger HQ, and all cheezfrends everywhere but espeshully these ones:

ANYTHING U CAN DUZ, I CAN DUZ BETTER.

LOLcat

hmm...u no,that iz an intrestin thery....but ur rong.
Shakespeare Kitten dost not approve of thou foul grammar
Gud ting 1 uv u iz docter, cauz u gon need medicul atenshun
I's sorry fax not s'port thesis
backseat driver kitteh. PICK A LANE JERKFACE!
Les try again frm 44. Wach my tail dis time for accellerando ppl.
OK, once again, 12345 is not a good password
Recipe for success SHOULD be here sumwhere...
Humans have no idea how to properly use a basket
I shredded all ur filez. data safe now
Hao much yoo pai for doze art lessuns? Can yoo gets reefund?
nao, abowt yor employment...it appeers dat micdonuldz is hiring,
...an they provide a family discownt
Well, if you had read the directions like I told you
then we wouldn't be in this mess now would we?
I put ded sqwerel in bag in case U want snak on plane.

RULES 2 NOM BY

LOLcat

Is whipped cream & shaved chocolate just too much to expect from you?
Bring me a frooty drink....wif a bendy straww.
Ur offering is grossly inadiquitz. And iz pink

Thx to

Jason A. Roberts
His lordship Börjesson and minions
Boston by Lauren & Will P.
"Tristan nomming my research paper" by Alison A. Cobian
Pictured: Ansel Davis [byansel.com] and Steve Davis. Photo by: cyndidavis.com
Nutmeg, by Robert Beardsell
Chopper by Momo and Hector www.youtube.com/miffychopper
Stinky by Lisa Jewell Michael
Larry by L. Barnum
Skiffle by Gillian F. Taylor
Mischa by Alexandra Radomsky & Josh Morrison
Mango by Mike
Nibbler by Anthony & Mallory Petronzi

Sofie by Sara B. and Matthew Marinelli

Thx to

Lulu by Catherine Smith
Willard by Shellme
Figit by Jena Hilston
Figit is a lovable, laid-back cat, whose favorite activities include
playing with his many toys, going for walks outside, and overdosing
on catnip. He is pampered and spoiled by his mother, Jena, whose life
wouldn't be the same without him. Figit also has two brothers, black
cats named Junior and Tippo.

hmm...no burds in dis tree. OK, cut down the next one.

You apparently haven't heard the story of how my previous human died.

We reazonable zombys Will take toona instead. Iz totaly fine.

I ordered a latte not a house blend

Sum sez haff full. Sum sez haff emtee. I sez haff MINE. Uther haff mine too.

This is satisfactory...I mean I expected bigger...

I vote tuna salad!

eeeeeexelent! What are u guys having?

Hasnt u got enny noms dat nawt green?

I will be supervising your shopping trip
Makes shur you get the right cat treats this time.

Oh, what? You're not done with this? Coulda sworn.

AROUND TEH HOUSE
LOLcat

You look upset. Did the children make another mess?

WHOAH! I have to admit ... that is DEFINITELY a huge spider! Okay, okay, calm down now ... and bring me your shotgun.

Bob Vila cat sayz...Applies the stain like dis ...

You really need to clean my litter box more often.

You sayz this iz ur seat? We sayz cry me a river.

Whaddaya mean why dident ai tell u dey were towin ur car? AI DID!!!

Ai sed "meow mew meow meow meow" and u just looked at meh and smiled.

iz in ur bowl improving ur 'fung shui'

one pillow for me one pillow for tail

Um...we needz tu hab a tawk bowt yur howsekeepin habits.

Don't ask me! I cough it up, you clean it up – that's the arrangement.

Why can't you ever talk about the times I DON'T destroy the toilet paper?!
You never mention THOSE!

Itty Bitty Kitty Committee Alumni Reunion by Rahel Jaskow
Elsie by Dave Gardner and Stacy Cannon
Karma, Mokie & Cheetah furrbals by Alicia & Don McDonald
Daisy by Matthew Clement
Handy by hello2kitteh
Sass by Scott Thomas
Miles by Amy Paul
"Earl Grey meets Chicken," by Kate Flint
Sophie by Angie Davidson (www.sophiecat.co.uk)
Walter by Brian and Kathy

Tobias Töffel by Thorsten (aka "kahless") and Rebecca (aka "clarissa06")

Thx to

Vinvella Alaqua von Woodward by Elizabeth Moore of Janesville, WI
Loki aka the "Furry Alarm Clock" by Sandra Chung
"Lights, Camera, Still Shots and Action" at sandra.redbubble.com
Gertie, by Jane Mickelborough
Ophelia by Alyssara
Crash + Burn - by Amanda Loos
Felicity Goodrich

Loki by his staff, Kelly & Pat Whyte
Mr. Last Chance Coe by Scott C. Coe
Zoe Moon
Trixie by Jane Terrell
Elsie by Dave Gardner and Stacy Cannon

Dog was wet. But iz ok, I takes care of it for you.

You can tell it's bad when the cat feels motivated to clean…

No. No more vacuum. Not ever.

to keeps fur off teh couch? Why yu tink dey calls it FURniture?

All dis plasticks gonna be nasty in teh summer. Jus sayin is all.

We would like to have a word with you about this new generic cat litter.

Lumbar kitteh is being supportive

Crime scene sheets. Freaky.

Why does my red carpet end here?

Set for Fluff Pleze

Queschun iz, did change com to mai literbox?

Ugh. If you didn't buy such hideous upholstery, I wouldn't have to shred it.

Dude. A VCR? You do know what year it is, right?

Kitteh bed wit tail extenshun? u finally did good hooman

Well? Are going to clean that up?

Nekst tyme yu goez owt kan yu pik me up a deeper pan? Dis wun nawt sooted tu mai purrpusses.

wot u mean drawer 4 u? U no fit!

LOOKIN' GUD

LOLcat

I'z on ur fork helpin u keep ur rezolooshuns.

Don't hate me cuz I bootyful Hate me cuz I throwd up on ur bed

You certainly have a lot of beauty products for someone of your … appearance.

Thank Gawd teh odder bridezmaidz also stuk wearin teh same lilac loser dress.

Kitteh fashul: furst wi exfoiliate an din follow up wit a gud toner.

We'll lick ur pore problum in no tiem.

You aksually wear dis?

Buddha by Joy Baisden
Boomer by Ruth Waterfield & Joe Fontana
Felix by Vicki Nadsady
Pootie, Baby Kitty, Anubis & Vincent and Erin Gerardi
Jasmine By Lady Lisa (Tina LaBlanc)
Jasmine is 1 of 4 rescued kittehs and also lives with a rescued goggie. Moar here: http://www.youtube.com/user/LadyLisaTabs. If you get hungry check out Lady Lisa's day job: http://www.harvestseasonings.com/ Waves, Hugz & Smootchies!

Yoda & his minions (um siblings) by Sheona Moore
Ishy sharing "his" chair with owner Sherri Photo by Nathan Williams
"Wu" by Andrea Otto
Shnookums Owns Everything by Tambobwe
Angel by MaryAnn Conner
Millie by Matt Slinger
Puck's Refusal by Sarah Patton
Photographer: Christopher B. Romeo / Model: George
Helvis Ostermeier
Weedog by Sheila Nelson
Mischief Mistoffolees by Mike
Clyde by Rebecca and Carl C

Thx to

Kerry Knight
Murph by Pepe Lepew
Zorro by Claire Louise Norton
Shadow by Sarah Law
Curious George by Tal & Carrie Shaked

Tigger and his hooman Vivienne House. Pic by Vicki House

To join me for tea you must change out of those jeans.
You can have pizza rolls or you can have spandex pants but you can't have both.
Trust me on this one.

ETIKET- ETTIQUET- UR DOIN IT RONG
LOLcat

Iz not bosseh I jus noe whut u shudz b doin
SILENCE! If I want your opinion, I'll give it to ya! Now hush, or I'll bop ya on the noggin.

Hoomin? Why have you closed that door? You know very well that you're not supposed to close any doors in my house. Unless of course it is to keep the dog outside. But I don't hear any whining on the other side of this door, so this is clearly a case of unauthorized door-closing on your part. You will rectify this situation immediately.
Your cat goddess awaits her sacrifice--the dog and gerbil should do nicely
Diet Kitteh...silently judges you
But I've played with these once, I need NEW toys.

Okai, we can do dis one ov two wayz. MY way, or da scratchey, bleedy, use-up-all-da-band-aidz way. I lets U chooz cause either wai iz cool wif me.
silence hooman iz tired of ur voice
Will you watch what you're doing next time you slam a door?
There could be people behind it, you know, trying to sleep!
Amish cat does not approve of your fancy washing machine
come wit me stupid human
Toylit Kitteh Maekin Shur yew wipe AND flush
Like you need another soda...Drink water, human.

eco kitteh frowns on your carbon footprint
'scuse me, but do AH post UR drunk pics on the interwebs?
Hullo...I iz ur nu AA sponsor...Go ahed, reach 4 ber...
Yu read dis one... Den go back to da bookstore and getz me a copy of "Dummies for Kittens" so eberybuddy will be up to speed, k?

Steven's Party by Samuel & Maria Cruz
"Microwave Mickey" by Heather and Lauree Little

Thx to

Elsie by Dave Gardner and Stacy Cannon
Photo: Barbara Talia
Cat: Maxwell
"Stewie" by Drew Lucas

Sr. Pitito by Annalucia Chong & Julia Costa
Fluffy by Beau & Vikki Edgington
Snoopy is owned by Betty and Doug Davis. She is part lilac point Siamese and is very photogenic. The cute caption was done by Kathrine Schwartman, aka momofzoo, who happens to have a dog named Snoopy.
Salem by Cassandra Bracero

Morris by Darian Anslow
Ceilidh by Robin Spittal

Gracie by Donna & Kevin Klabunde
Bebe by Laura and Eismantas Vaitiekūnai
Falstaff by Ginger Yarger
Photo of Saint, by Daniel Camacho. Pleez to vizit Saint at Bear Creek Feline Center, Panama City, FL.. www.bearcreekfelinecenter.org (850) 722-9927
Hazel by Claire & Kenna White
Kiwi Katface by Emily
Susi by Karel, Lara & Nadia B.
Braveheart by Debbie Siemering

FREE TIME

LOLcat

DIS YER NEW SKEDULE. PINK MEANZ YU FEEDZ MEH, 'N GREEN ONEZ ARE CHOREZ: CLEAN'N' LITTERBOX, PETTIN' ME 'N STUUFFZ LIK DAT

If you insist on surfing the internet before feeding me, might I suggest you Google "scars and lacerations, emergency treatment."

Study? Wut u meen study? U pay attenshun to only meh. Its the rules. No study.

Iz teim we talkd...bout ur Depp addickshun.

Bridezilla cat wants alternations done NAO!

OH NOES – TEH NEKKID YOGA AGIN.

I am more important than anything that happens in your human world anyway.

Dumbledore dies. nao feedz me!

Ya know, if we could just agree on this "no baths" thing you'd be able to take the paramedics off speed dial.

U stop playin now Is food and hugs tiem.

I didz ironing. U cleen box & make noms?

unhealthy interests u has them.

Thank you for covering me up but now if you could turn off the light and sing to me.

Ai halps wif ur projekt knit 1, purrl 1, nom awl teh rests!

we'z gonna make smorz & swim nekkid & stay up all night talking, k?

Really...this is what you do all day. u doin it rong

Hoomin, pleez, come heer and hand me my ball

K, I beleeves I haz FINALLY had nuff petting. Yuz kin stopz now.......hello?

Yep. As usual, you're doing diddly squat.

Why iz I not part of your planz today?

I get to be the shoe, or NOBODY plays

Thx to

Cody-ody-ody-ody GCHLoki

Marcipan by Blanka Lanszki

Seamus by Kelly Russell
Captain Jack by Tessa & Cory Cox and Sam Kowalczyk
Niblet by: Amber, Chris & Lily Koenig. Hi, Megan P!
Stella by Anna Letko
Ellie by John & Terrie Scott
Tipper by Aleta McDaniel
Checkers — our furbaby by Daniel & Abigail Patterson

Liddle Morticia, 9 weeks, by Maddy Nish
Pretty Girl by Andy Hilal & Julia Lam
Sweetie by Milly Bays A.K.A Candace
Rūdis of Murrdor
Alice by Hillary & Melinda White
Colebertini by Sean & Kate Edmonds
Cab & Doolin: Photo by Laura T. Ryan
Jess by Stephen, Jacquie, Joshua & Joel
Pixel by Ed Toton
"Gamer Kitten" by Alecia Burke
Squeaky by Mark and Terri
B.C. (Bad Cat) by Laurel

RELASHUNS
LOLcat

Girlfrend dumpt you, sorry. So... whas teh protocol for eating ex-girlfriends fud?
Chastity Cat ish protecting your daughters
Could be worse...You culd haz a boyfrind or a huzband or sumfin!
Don't give meh that "cootchy coo" crap—YOU'RE LATE WITH MY NOMS!
Weave diskussed dis, and u dont haf to muv out.
Iz never havin kids. theyz poopin, theyz cryin....theyz hasselin the kitteh...
Yeah, I'm really sorry that loser left ya...but u cudda least saved me a taste a this.
Now please allow me to bite a mouse in half and smoosh it against your lips.
I did the Math. we can't afford the Dog
kitteh heers your cries for help n kitteh is indifferent to them
DON'T LET THIS HAPPEN TO YOU! Please have your human spayed or neutered.
Haven't you done enough already?

UP CLOSE AND PURRSONAL
LOLcat

I like yu. Yur nawt veree brite, but yu tryz hard. Nao go fech me sum toona.
Hey...don't cry!!! I mock everyone—I'm a cat, it's my job!!!
share cheezburger or face continued stink-eye
The next time you feel like "bonding," superglue yourself to the wall.
annoying neighbor kitteh Ur yard haz weedz, Ur musik iz too loud, an Ur dog poopz in my yard!
You iz awake? I need nomz.
You really need to learn to pace your naps, like I do. Just last week alone, you missed our 3am playtime twice and would have slept through Sunday if I hadn't pounced on your face.
Um, yu do kno dat depweshun is jist anger wifowt enfuziazm, rite?
Dis wat u look like after party.
so, are you going to share that or do i have to slap you again?
Liv evry day az if yu will die tumorrow Cuz it kan be arranjed

Thx to

Lola with Will by Chris Schmied
Lucy by Pawel Ryszka
Sarina Wayne @ www.thecats.com
Mashka by Tatiana Alexandrovitch (on the picture, Mashka and Anna Alexandrovitch)
Pyewacket & Pouncequick by Chantelle Giguere
Whoop Whoop and Lucy by Vicki & Tim Peterson
Mrs. Dash, a.k.a. Doodle-Bug, by Laura D Borders
Alex, by Melissa Titcomb
El Chunko by Yolanda Allen
Smudge by Alex and Sara. Hands by Stephanie.
Giger by James and Jess Boyer
Zaire Duck & Zoe Goose by Alia & Stacie

Thx to

Tiger Pardue, son of Linda & Tom by Scion of Insanity
Amanda & Mike D'Onofrio Picture of Simon Talsma
Snopuff, owner of John Berry
Rain Disapproves by GnashArts.com
Eefje by Tessa16
Stevie Los Banos
Phoebe by Laura and Alicia

Vladimir by JoDee Bebernes
Sulis Minerva by Heather Bailie
Samus is continuously disappointed by Nathan and Ashley Acuff
Annebelle by Alyssa Goch

More awsumness for every1 (even hoomins) from teh LOLcats!

978-1-592-40409-4

978-1-592-40516-9

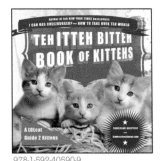

978-1-592-40590-9

On sale now!!1!